BUILT *for* STEALTH

Scott Allan is an international bestselling author of 25+ books published in 7 languages in the area of personal growth and self- development. He is the author of *Fail Big*, *Undefeated*, and *Do the Hard Things First*.

As a former corporate business trainer in Japan, and Transformational Mindset Strategist, Scott has invested over 10,000 hours of research and instructional coaching into the areas of self-mastery and leadership training.

With an unrelenting passion for teaching, building critical life skills, and inspiring people around the world to take charge of their lives, Scott Allan is committed to a path of constant and never-ending self-improvement.

Many of the success strategies and self-empowerment material that is reinventing lives around the world evolves from Scott Allan's 20 years of practice and teaching critical skills to corporate executives, individuals, and business owners.

You can connect with Scott at:
scottallan@scottallanpublishing.com
Visit author.to/ScottAllanBooks to stay up to date on future book releases.

More Bestselling Titles From Scott Allan

Empower Your Thoughts

Empower Your Deep Focus

Rejection Reset

Rejection Free

Relaunch Your Life

Drive Your Destiny

The Discipline of Masters

Do the Hard Things First

Undefeated

No Punches Pulled

Fail Big

Bite the Bullet

Supercharge Your Best Life

Visit author.to/ScottAllanBooks to follow Scott Allan and stay up to date on future book releases

BUILT *for* STEALTH

How to **BUILD** an **AWESOME** Life

SCOTT ALLAN

Published by
Rupa Publications India Pvt. Ltd 2023
7/16, Ansari Road, Daryaganj
New Delhi 110002

Sales Centres:
Prayagraj Bengaluru Chennai
Hyderabad Jaipur Kathmandu
Kolkata Mumbai

Copyright © Scott Allan 2023

The views and opinions expressed in this book are the author's own and the facts are as reported by him which have been verified to the extent possible, and the publishers are not in any way liable for the same.

All rights reserved.
No part of this publication may be reproduced, transmitted, or stored in a retrieval system, in any form or by any means, electronic, mechanical, photocopying, recording or otherwise, without the prior permission of the publisher.

P-ISBN: 978-93-5702-147-0
E-ISBN: 978-93-5702-148-7

First impression 2023

10 9 8 7 6 5 4 3 2 1

Printed in India

This book is sold subject to the condition that it shall not, by way of trade or otherwise, be lent, resold, hired out, or otherwise circulated, without the publisher's prior consent, in any form of binding or cover other than that in which it is published.

CONTENTS

1. Built for Stealth: A Brief Overview — 1
2. 6 Steps to Begin Where You Are — 7
3. The 11 Traits of Epic Performers — 13
4. The 8-Step Formula for Breaking Bad Habits — 22
5. 7 Ways for Mastering Failure — 30
6. The 7-Step Framework for Continuous Change — 42
7. Control Distractions and Manage Shiny Object Syndrome — 50
8. 7 Ways to Retrain Your Brain — 57
9. 5 Steps to Leveraging Fear (and Becoming Your Best) — 70
10. 7 Tips for Handling Rejection Sensitivity — 76
11. Breaking Through Obstacles: A 4-Step Formula — 86
12. What It Takes to Win (and Master Your Greatest Gift) — 100
13. How to Create Purpose for Your Life — 108
14. Develop Your Obsession (and do whatever it takes) — 116
15. The 6 Habits of Self-Control — 129
16. Built for Stealth: A Brief Conclusion — 144

"Success means doing the best we can with what we have. Success is the doing, not the getting; in the trying, not the triumph. Success is a personal standard, reaching for the highest in us, becoming all we can be."

—Zig Ziglar

BUILT FOR STEALTH: A BRIEF OVERVIEW

One of my core fundamental beliefs is that, a life well lived is built on a steady path towards progress. I believe that progress is, as Tony Robbins said, "the only measure of success."

It is this commitment to building an extraordinary life that builds drive, fuels momentum, and ignites your passion to do hard things even when you don't feel like doing them.

The second pillar strength is building identity. I talk about this in Built for Stealth, but I must bring it up here at the beginning of our journey together. Your identity—the values you hold to be true for yourself—form the core of everything that is possible.

When you believe it's possible, you make it possible

The promises you make to yourself will form key habits that build repetition. And what you repeat, you become. When you become a person of consistent repetition, and your actions move you towards a goal that you absolutely must have, every small win gradually racks up to deliver the big prize later.

Your commitment, hard work, determination and resilience comes together to forge a bulletproof way of life that raises the stakes across every area of your life: Your personal relationships, your business, and your dreams come together to form a tight unit.

One of the greatest statements you can begin using for yourself is: "I'm the type of person that (action statement) …."

"I'm the type of person that does whatever it takes." "I'm the type of person that works hard until I achieve my goals."

"I'm the type of person that takes care of my friends and family."

Your identity statements are powerful, and as you move through this book, begin every day by repeating five identity statements first thing in the morning.

A successful life always begins with your mind, and creating an identity for the type of person you are aiming to become begins with being that person right now.

With these lessons, let's move into the framework and learn the strategies that create change and fuel momentum.

Your Success Roadmap in 30 minutes a day or less

I love to learn and push beyond the limitations my mind has set. We all have limits, and most of these are self-imposed limits built on the lies we have been telling ourselves since way back when.

As an author, I have made it my mission to help people break through the barriers of rejection, fear, and misguided beliefs that keep us stuck. You are probably living a life far below your potential, and my purpose with creating books, journals and courses is to provide for you with an all-purpose training platform. Think of this as your education into another world, and you are the master architect of this world. You decide how you want everything to look and feel.

You create opportunity instead of just waiting for it to happen. You build the path that you want to take instead of treading on the path already taken. You learn from failure instead of avoiding failure and doing nothing. You become the best version of yourself and hold to your highest values instead of someone else deciding who you should be.

Yes, you can create this kind of life for yourself from today and all the days to follow.

I want you to succeed. If you're here, you want the same thing: To become the most excellent version of yourself that exceeds any self-imposed expectations you may be holding onto.

Imagine—for the next five minutes—your life as it unfolds in the next ten years. How do you want it to materialize? What is the story you're building for yourself? What experiences do you visualize having? How is your dream going to be realized? What are you willing to do to make it happen?

"You can only fail if you fail yourself. You become unstoppable by tapping into your hidden abilities and discovering what you are truly capable of. This is the path to empowering your life, success, and everything in between."

Don't wait for the opportunity to arrive. There is a difference between being patient and expecting change to occur without having to take intentional action. Real change—the chances you create through action—happens as you aim for a goal that's almost impossible to hit.

The goal is to turn your vision—your dream—into a tangible lifestyle. In all of my work and teachings, everything is centered around clarity of purpose. Knowing what you want and then doing whatever it takes to get it. I don't teach quick gimmicks or how to succeed with a straightforward strategy overnight.

I provide real-world action plans that get tangible results through consistent massive action. I believe in results that are sustainable. It's not just about rah-rah and feeling good but taking intentional action and feeling great from the successful results and outcome you want.

The strategies in this book provides a detailed map that directs your focused attention in the right direction.

How to Read *Built for Stealth*

Built for stealth is a compilation of the best frameworks that I've created to help epic achievers—just like you—push beyond personal boundaries and break past self- imposed limitations. The chapters in **Built for Stealth** have been adapted from some of the best strategies taught throughout my books, courses and personal training.

You can begin from chapter 1 and read the book from front to back. Or, choose a chapter to read per day in any order. I do recommend beginning with chapter 1: 6

Steps to Begin Where You Are. From there, feel free to pick and choose the lessons that align with your area of interest. You can also download the audiobook here and, listen to *Built for Stealth* when you're on the move.

The framework for **Built For Stealth** is made up of these key principles as they appear in the book:

- 6 Steps to Begin Where You Are
- The 11 Traits of Epic Performers
- The 6-Step Formula for Breaking Bad Habits

- Master the Influence of Failing Big
- The 7-Step Framework for Continuous Change
- Control Distractions and Manage Shiny Object Syndrome
- 7 Ways to Retrain Your Brain
- 5 Simple Steps to Leveraging Fear (and Becoming Your Best)
- 7 Tips for Handling Rejection Sensitivity
- What It Takes to Win (and Master Your Greatest Gift)
- How to Create Purpose for Your Life
- Develop Your Obsession (and do whatever it takes)

Join me on this journey as I walk you through each of the principles here and, how you can apply this blueprint to your own life.

You are the architect of your own destiny and stacking the building blocks for your life begins with the first step.

If you're ready, it's time to take that step forward. Let's begin.

Scott Allan

"Success is not measured by what you accomplish, but by the opposition you have encountered, and the courage with which you have maintained the struggle against overwhelming odds."

—Orison Swett Marden

6 STEPS TO BEGIN WHERE YOU ARE

"A year from now you may wish you had started today."

—Karen Lamb

Most people fail to get anywhere with their goals because they fail to start anything. They sit and wait, getting stuck in too many details, leading to feelings of overwhelm. This brings fear of failure and stirs up memories of things you started in the past…and gave up.

You negotiate with your mind and decide now is not the time. The excuses step in. You tell yourself "I'll wait until…"

- "I'm financially stable."
- "The conditions are better than they are now."
- "My kids are older, and I have more time."
- "I feel more confident than I am now."

The excuses hold you back and you never actually start anything. If you want to start, you must begin. If you write nothing down on the blank page, it stays blank until you put pen to paper. Write one word. Just one. Then write another one. Make it a sentence.

Sounds too simple? You just started something. You begin

everything by taking that first step, no matter how easy it is.

What are you waiting for? The perfect day to start, the best weather conditions, or that day when you're feeling your best and totally unbeatable.

Conditions are subject to change. The best time to begin your life was yesterday. The next best time is now. No matter what your conditions are—rich or broke, sad or happy, ready or not—we are going to begin right NOW.

Make your decision to stop waiting and start doing. Turn off the TV. Move into silence and prepare your mind for what is coming.

It doesn't matter where you are at in your life right now, how much you've failed, or how hopeless your situation appears right now. No matter where you are, who you are, how much you've failed in the past, you can start from where you're at. It's never too late to succeed or make tomorrow better than today, and today better than yesterday.

Procrastination is a fantasy that you can defeat with simple action tasks built into your routine. If procrastination is holding you back, and you're making excuses why you can't begin now, do the simplest thing imaginable.

For years I put off filling out an application form I had to get done. But I knew it was a long process and I hate applications. So one day I asked myself, "What is the simplest thing I can do to get this started?"

I wrote my name on the application. Then the date. Within an hour, I had completed most of it. I waited three years to do something that could have been done in less than an hour.

Don't wait. You'll regret it. Begin your journey with me today.

As Mark Twain once said, ""The secret of getting ahead is getting started."

So, let's get started. Begin where you are. With what you have. Right now. With who you are.

Getting Started: Action Steps

1. **Put together a plan.** Plan your work, and then work your plan! You have to know your destination before you set out on for the journey, or at the very least, know what direction you want to travel in. The plan you build is your blueprint for the future; be sure to include all-important concepts and make detailed steps for each part of the journey.
2. **Gather necessary information or resources.** This is a powerful way to get started on your plan. Go to the Internet, check out the yellow pages, or visit the library to collect any information you need that starts the momentum moving. Having knowledge or specific information before you jump right into it could save you time and wasted effort down the road.
3. **Break it down into manageable chunks.** One of the reasons we procrastinate over starting something new is the size of the workload that is in front of us. When you are standing in front of the world's tallest mountain, it appears to be an insurmountable obstacle in your past.

    If you have a project, a goal, or something that needs to be done, thinking of it as a whole creates in many people a fear of actually doing anything. Garages and basements remain in disarray; important work is discarded half way through; books and paintings go unfinished; and the ability to actually finish anything becomes a daunting task.

4. **Make Important Contacts.** One of the obstacles that gets in the way of taking *Immediate Action* is having to make the appropriate contacts with people that can actually help us to achieve success. I have lost some very good opportunities in the past simply because I didn't follow through with contacting the people that could have steered me in the right direction.

   If there is a group or even a mentor you know you should contact that could feed you advice on your current situation, contact them immediately. Even if you don't require their services just yet, by taking that first initial step, you are putting the wheels in motion.

5. **Stop talking about it; just Do It!** Have you ever found yourself talking about doing something over and over again only months or years later realize you still hadn't gotten around to it? Well, if so, you are not alone.

   Everyone has done this at least one point in their lives; they have good intentions of doing the action they have been talking about, but just never really *'getting around to it.'* People might have even hinted that all you do is talk, but never produce, like a chicken that spends all day squawking but lays no eggs.

   The truth is, people don't respond to cheap words of what you want to do. They might listen to you once when you tell them you are going to do this and that, but the fact is, action speaks louder than words. It always has, and it always will.

   It is perfectly ok to tell people about something you are

thinking about doing or have wanted to do for a long time, but if years later you are still saying the same thing, you will eventually stop listening to yourself, and others will stop listening to you as well. Be a person that gets things done, not just for others, but for yourself!
6. **Implement the 5-Second Rule.** This strategy comes from world-class speaker Mel Robbins, author of the book *The 5 Second Rule* and the *High Five Habit*. How it works is simple. When you catch yourself holding back from getting started on anything, you count down from five and follow these three steps.

5...4...3...2...1...

1. **Breathe deeply.** Breathing has many benefits, and when you take a deep breath, hold it for three seconds and release it, you are letting go of the energy that keeps you stuck.
2. **Do the most straightforward thing possible.** This could be flipping open your laptop or picking up a pencil. Whatever it is, you take the most straightforward action to build momentum. Momentum is energy in motion, and getting it churning, begins with the first step.
3. **Commit to ten minutes of work. That's it.** You don't have to do this for an hour or overcommit for the day. Only ten minutes and you're on your way to beginning that task you have been putting off.

Let's do a short exercise. Choose something you have meant to start but haven't found the time. Is your house a mess? A musical instrument you want to play? Going to the gym to exercise? A project on your to-do list for the past five years?

Whatever it is, **write it down** now. Okay, ready?

Take the most straightforward step possible to get moving.

- Are you writing an important email? Write the first sentence.
- Do you want to exercise? Start stretching and doing light weights at home.
- Are you cleaning your house? Start by picking up things and putting them intoAre you learning
- Learning to play guitar? Practice one chord only.
- Are you learning to type? Sign up for a free online course that shows the basics. Take the first lesson.

Don't even think too long or hard about what you're going to do. Just do *something*. Get started.

After 10 minutes, stop and check how you feel. Do you feel excited and motivated to continue?

Many people think they must be 'motivated' to begin. But that's not how it works. Motivation only comes through doing something first. The motivation to continue follows through with your action.

Even if it's something that will take you months or years to complete, taking that first step gives you momentum. Instead of wasting time just *thinking* about it, you can start doing it whenever you want. You can do this for anything. Try it with a priority task that will change how you feel.

Action task: Just Begin Now

Set a timer for 10 minutes. During this time, you will focus on your task and only this one thing. You can use this daily when you take action toward a priority task. You can only become good at something when you do it often.

THE 11 TRAITS OF EPIC PERFORMERS

*"No matter what he does, every person on earth
plays a central role in the history of the world.
And normally he doesn't know it."*

—Paulo Coelho

When you look at the long list of epic performers around the world, there is a definitive list of traits that sets them apart from mediocre results. But the illusion that most of us believe in is that epic performers—Jeff Bezos, Oprah Winfrey, Steven Spielberg, Steve Jobs—were born with a genius and gifts that you and I just don't have.

Although genetics does play a role, it's not the deciding factor in who gets to perform at a level that stretches into the extraordinary. By modeling the traits of epic performance, you and I can level the playing field and create our own version of success.

Here is a concise list of epic performance traits that the world-class share regarding achieving dynamic results. And you can also achieve great results by adapting the best trait of dynamic performers.

1. Epic performers have clear, concise goals, in line with their greatest passion

They know exactly what they want. This level of clarity on our goals I what drives us to take consistent action, no matter what the circumstances are.

With your goals in clear sight, and an actionable plan for how you'll get there, you can turn anything into a positive result with the implementation of an actionable plan.

If you have a goal you can't stop thinking about, if it keeps you awake at night, then you need to act on it. Turn your obsession into reality by making it real.

Tell people about your goal. You have to share this with people. Even if they don't act interested, they will pay attention when the changes in your life become obvious. Instead of asking you, "Are you sure you should be doing this?", people will start asking, "How did you do that?".

What are you most passionate about? What is the one idea that occupies your thoughts continuously? How can you inject this passion into achieving your life's vision right now?

2. Epic performers have a concrete plan, supported by actionable habits

Anyone—whether in business or sports—who has ever overcome any difficult obstacle or achieved a great accomplishment did so with a specific plan, supported by a clear plan of action.

You must be clear in your actions and intentions. You can have good intentions, but without following through, you will only defeat yourself and eventually, return to the same place you were before: Stuck.

These habits may include eating the right foods to get into better shape. If you are in the habit of eating junk food, but you know you need to change this, then adopt the habit of eating more fruits and vegetables. By implementing consistent habits, you can achieve your goal of losing weight and running a marathon or joining a triathlon.

Begin with your goal and work out the actionable habits you need to make it a reality. High-level achievers—people who get their work done—are using this strategy to win. You cannot be defeated if you have a goal driven by intentional action.

3. Epic performers are people who can navigate through insurmountable obstacles along the way

There will always be something blocking you from moving ahead. These are the obstacles that define who we are. You will learn what you are capable of when you can tackle any problem or challenge and find a solution to get around it. In any business or personal goal, you will be challenged to prove what you are capable of.

This isn't something that should cause fear and hesitation; rather, embrace the chance to be your best and show the world you are here to win. Do you ever see people give up on something because it is "too difficult"? Anything in life worth having will not be easy to get. If it were, everyone would get what they want.

Take a moment and think about the obstacles in your life right now. Do you struggle with any self-defeating behaviors, negative thought patterns, or situations that have to be cleared before you can move forward?

Recognize and identify what could potentially hold you back. Then, identify the one action you can take now—even if it is something small—that will push you to confront and overcome this obstacle. Your thoughts are the fulcrum that moves all things.

4. Epic performers are positive in their approach and develop the right mindset to finish what they start

Commitment is the key to winning. Look at someone who sets out with a goal in mind and achieves that goal, even when it's years—or decades—later.

Let's look at Ben, for example, someone who started an online business with his wife a little over 10 years ago. They knew from the start they had to put in a certain number of hours per week to get the business off the ground.

They had the passion, the drive, and a plan to launch the business within one year. By committing to a weekly action plan they set for themselves, they created a system whereby they were each responsible for a specific part of the business.

Commitment means sticking with your dream when faced with hard times. You might go through a financial crisis, you might lose your business partner, or a personal disaster might occur, but the committed mind will transcend all obstacles and find a way to finish the race.

5. Epic performers can visualize the outcome they want and continue to push ahead until they get there

A commitment to your dream, and a strategy to take massive action, are followed by a vision of what you strive to accomplish. Everything in your life—whether it succeeds or fails—can be traced back to the vision you hold for your life, and the environment you desire to create.

No vision means a good chance of failing or ending up in some place you don't want to be, because you followed someone else's plan.

You can begin with the end in mind. Visualize your life at the end, and the level of happiness you will have achieved in your life.

When you visualize the outcome of your plan, your mind works to formulate the necessary actions needed. By consciously visualizing the course of action needed, your mind will formulate the steps necessary to take you there.

By knowing ahead of time what needs to be done to reach your destination, you will build momentum in your actions and enhance your enthusiasm to keep pushing ahead.

"Starting strong is good. Finishing strong is epic."

—Robin Sharma

6. Epic performers are strategic in their approach to the work

Purpose-driven people are committed to working diligently toward their dreams with actionable intent. They organize all activities, thoughts, and actions toward defining this singleness of purpose. They have an organized plan for achieving everything they set out to do. The individual with a purpose-driven mind has a list of actionable items that must be completed, according to the objectives they are working toward.

This strategic mindset toward work is a defining trait you should develop from now. By being strategic, preparing ahead, and utilizing every minute for maximum efficiency, you can work less time but be just as effective.

What actions could you take every day that would have a significant impact on your life one month from now?

What actions could you start doing tomorrow that would change everything if you continued this course for 90 days? Instead of following someone else's plan for your life, what is a plan you could create in alignment with your passions and objectives?

Let's take an example. If you are building a house, and you want to finish it in three months, how much time would you have to allocate to this project each day?

If you break down all the various projects into tasks and allocate an estimated time frame to each of these tasks, then you can crush each piece of work systematically. Set a mini-goal to achieve just one task a day.

7. Epic performers have realistic expectations built around a predictable outcome

One of the reasons people set themselves up for failure is, they have unrealistic expectations for what they can achieve.

Remember what Tony Robbins said: *"We overestimate what*

we can do in a month but underestimate what can be achieved in a year."

You have to be realistic about what is possible when you start working toward a goal. If you decide to run a full marathon, but you can barely make it to the 5k mark, you will have to run for several months and build up to it.

This takes time. Likewise, when setting up a business, there is a lot to learn, and you will make mistakes along the way. Failing on the journey I the process. Pick yourself up when you get knocked down, and keep moving forward.

Be prepared for setbacks. Not everything will go according to plan. Most of it won't, so part of having realistic expectations is knowing what you are capable of and how long your projected goal may take.

People who end up defeated often had expectations beyond what was possible. After not meeting their expectations, they feel deflated and convince themselves that they are a complete failure, but that is not the case. You have to reset your expectations and realize that being realistic about what can be done right now is part of the formula.

8. Epic performers are persistent in the face of defeat.

People committed to the "*Undefeated* Lifestyle" do not give up, surrender, or give in to failure. They perceive failure as a necessary pathway to a successful outcome. Failure is the road to success. Persistence plays a vital role in succeeding at anything you have a desire to accomplish. For successful people, facing that failure and overcoming their fears to break through obstacles is the only path to winning.

What obstacles do you face now? Are these barriers going to stop you from living your life as it could be lived?

Look at an obstacle in your life that is slowing your progress and map out a list of solutions you can apply today to begin working through it.

Take the best solution and put it into action. If it doesn't work, try another solution. Keep working on this, until you have overcome this surmountable barrier. Often, most obstacles that defeat you are bigger in your mind than they really appear.

9. Epic performers have a superior belief system

Successful people have unshakable faith in what they can achieve; they believe in their mission, ideas, and importance of purpose. Regardless of obstacles or challenges, they are confident that anything can be overcome, if they believe it can be. They have the foundational belief that they will succeed, overcome any obstacle, and do anything to see the outcome they desire come to fruition.

Most people set limits on themselves because of limiting beliefs. They create limited income, decide they have limited abilities, and create limited learning skills.

However, successful people are limitless in their pursuits. They continue to grow, expand, develop, and reach out to breach the horizons untouched by the masses.

What do you believe in? Do you believe success is a matter of luck or chance? Or, do you believe that anything can happen if you believe in the possibilities? Your beliefs—like your habits—forge a powerful alliance with destiny.

10. Epic performers do things most people avoid

Albert E.N. Gray, author of the *New Common Denominator of Success*, said:

> *"Successful people are successful because they form the habits of doing those things that failures don't like to do."*

This is the most defining characteristic that separates people who do what they love to do from those who do what they are made to do by others.

People who do things most people are afraid of live life as an expression of the choices they have made. Your actions define you. Do what needs to be done for as long as it takes, and you will have very little competition.

Is there an action you have been avoiding because you're afraid of failing, or the road appears to be too difficult, so you procrastinate? Remember, whatever your purpose in this life may be, you will have a much better chance to live life your way when you do things most people would turn away from.

Right now, make a short list of three actions you can take this week that will have a major impact on your performance. Then, from that list of five actions, choose only one of them and focus on it for 30 days. Make this action the key to pushing your momentum to its peak.

THE 8-STEP FORMULA FOR BREAKING BAD HABITS

Your habits play an important role in your success. We already know this, but the challenge comes in knowing which habits are good and which damage our lifestyle.

Habits aren't good or bad unless they hold you back from achieving what you truly desire in your life.

A system of negative habits may be defeating you in many ways, and they are not always so obvious. If it is something you've been doing for a long time, there is no doubt you get a reward or pleasure from your habits.

Some of these habits could include:

- Watching TV just to numb out and escape
- Texting people you don't know just to avoid loneliness
- Eating junk food
- Worrying about things that might never happen
- Staying up too late
- Procrastinating (about everything)

If you want better health, obviously eating excessive amounts of junk food or smoking would be categorized as bad habits. Charles Duhigg, bestselling author of *The Power of Habit*, said: *The Golden Rule of Habit Change: You can't extinguish a bad habit, you can only change it.*

If we can't discern the good from the bad, we end up taking actions without thinking about what we are working for. When you climb the wrong ladder, it doesn't matter if you reach the top or not. This same principle applies to building better habits to put us on a more focused path.

In my years of experience, I have seen people continue to perform poorly, not from lack of skill or knowledge, but because they had poor habits that set them up for failure.

The problem is that we don't know what we don't know, and when it comes to habit formation, we don't know which habits are helping us and which are hurting us. Even sometimes when it feels like we are doing the right thing, that habit can be hurting our chances of getting ahead.

Our passive habits make us afraid to take action. These habits are automatic, and we feed them repeatedly throughout the day without any conscious effort. Passive habits may include:

- Sleeping in late because that is what you have always done.
- Spending money you don't have when you're bored.
- Watching TV for hours to avoid working.
- Scrolling through social media feeds looking for something interesting to entertain you.
- Eating junk food without any thought about how we will feel the next day.

What bad habits can you replace with good ones? What is it you hope to achieve with this new arrangement?

The Habits that Keep You Scared

For years, I had several habits that kept me scared and trapped. Procrastination was at the top of the list. I was always in the habit of neglecting what needed to be done. For example, creating a life plan, a financial plan, or mapping out my goals were all things I wanted to accomplish, but whenever I thought about them there was something more pressing to do.

Procrastination, while it felt like I was in control because I could make the decision to do or not do something, was robbing me of the life I could have had. The habit of doing it later became destructive. And, because I wasn't getting the things done that should have been, I was always scared of the future. Will I be okay? What if I run out of money? What is going to happen to my life?

When you develop the right habits, fear has no place in your life. To feel positive and enthusiastic about the future, we need structure and an organized plan, even if it is only a temporary one. Whenever I tried to act on my bad habits they would lead back to more procrastination. Then I'd experience a deep sense of fear that had returned. Bad habits are those that hold you back from achieving the impossible. You'll never be great with mediocre habits.

Right now, identify three bad habits you'd like to kick. Once identified, ask yourself: *why is it important for me to replace these habits with something else?* Without a strong enough answer, chances are you'll struggle to succeed at replacing them and eventually slip back into old routines, do what you've always done, and get what you've always gotten.

Eight Steps for Breaking Bad Habits

Step 1: Recognize the Routine

Every habit has a place of origin. It thrives in a certain environment triggered by a stimulus. The routine is your way of feeding the habit. We give it what it desires the most: a reward. By feeding bad habits they are able to stay strong and control you.

A routine is a set of actions repeated consistently, often subconsciously. It is triggered by an external or internal stimulus in which we feel the need to feed this habit by giving into the impulse.

For most people, it is an addiction of some sort, such as smoking, checking email often, or compulsively shopping. Once you decide the course of action, it follows a set pattern and, if there is an emotional reward, you will continue to repeat the behavior.

Once you recognize the routine of your habit, you can implement a new set of actions to change it.

Step 2: Identify the Trigger

This is the point where we can catch our bad habit as it is stimulated by a trigger. This can be anything from an environmental trigger, watching something on TV, a feeling we suddenly get, or a certain person we meet.

The trigger, in this case, is the key. Once you identify what triggers you to take action, this is the point you are going to make a decision to either act…or not.

Your trigger is often an impulsive act. We don't think but

react when it is switched on. It's purely compulsive. Addictions are formed through triggers. When we can recognize the trigger approaching, such as a craving for doing something, it becomes easier to turn it around.

Step 3: Replace the Action and Create New Behavior

If you make the conscious choice to not act when the trigger is activated, you have to replace the intended action [how you would normally react] with a new action. This new pattern, if repeated and implementing the replacement action, will form the new habit over a matter of weeks or months.

Just using willpower alone to try and not act out isn't enough. If you bare-knuckle it, you'll never recover.

This is like an addict trying to kick the habit cold turkey without making attempts to replace the addiction. We need to know what the routine is, and then, when we are triggered to respond, be ready to take a different set of actions that break the habit.

For example: You might be triggered to buy something online because you are bored. How can you replace this? Step away from the computer as soon as the trigger hits you. Get busy with another activity. You could even shut down your computer for the night and do something else that will break the impulse.

Step 4: Cut away the one activity that is robbing you of your greatest resource: **TIME.** Do you watch too much TV? Waste time complaining? Compulsive shopping when you don't need anything?

Step 5: Focus on Small, Incremental Changes

Reframing a habit takes time. You won't reinvent all your habits right away, but you will if you repeatedly switch your triggers and make yourself aware of the areas in which you are weak.

If your habit is wasting time on social media when you could be doing more constructive things, create a plan and a system to move away from this habit. With so many distractions, wasting time on worthless activities is common.

The changes may be small, but any shift in your attitude, emotions, or actions is going to have a long-term impact if practiced consistently. This is how habits are formed, and this is how they can be reinvented.

Step 6: Create an action plan for the next 30 days

The goal is to commit to a set action plan for each day. This can be as simple as committing to five minutes per day doing a single action.

For example, if you're trying to build the exercise habit, you can do just five reps on the first day. If you are writing a book, commit to writing for 10 minutes a day for the next 30 days.

What matters isn't how much we get done. The idea is to follow through with the action and make it a consistent pattern you will perform every day, regardless of whether it is 10 reps or 50. You can scale up later, when you are conditioned to perform the action without thinking about it.

Step 7: Review your progress after 30 days.

How consistently did you follow through with the action? Did you miss any days?

How would you measure your success, compared to 30 days

ago? You can review your progress by asking yourself: "How do I feel now, compared to 30 days ago?" This is easy to map out. If you have been sticking with your course for 30 days, the progress is obvious.

Step 8: Focus on Your New Reward

There has to be a driving force behind change. Otherwise, what is the point? Earlier we talked about the Ostrich Approach and how we bury our heads in the sand to escape reality. This escape tactic is, in many ways, a reward for people.

We can avoid the current reality that is frightening, and live as if everything is just fine. But when we get real about what is actually happening in our lives and make changes, the rewards are revealed much later.

In the immediate gratification approach you might feel good now because you're seemingly getting away with: paying your bills, having a discussion, or accepting an illness. But, the immediate gratification approach has poor long-term rewards. In the end, you end up losing more than if you had taken action in the beginning.

To change a habit, you have to see the reward that is to come, but it might take months or years before you see any results. That's okay. If it were easy, everyone would be doing it.

Think of it this way: even though you might be scared to set up a financial plan for yourself, ten years from now, your family will be so much better off if you start today. Always have the reward serve as a reminder of what is yet to come. Don't let it go. Keep it there in the front of your mind at all times.

You can monitor your habit changing progress. Do this whenever a trigger moment occurs – when you are bored or meet someone that makes you want to react a certain way.

By not giving into this feeling, you have just gained points. Every time you say NO, it paves the way for a larger YES down the road.

When you create a journal, dedicate a section or page to one habit you are working on reinventing. Record your progress, changes made, and most of all, how you really feel about committing to this habit changing challenge.

Action Task:

Identify one bad habit you want to eliminate and implement the good habit that will take its place. Example: I will stop eating potato chips before bed and replace this with a salad.

Make a list of habits that are destroying your lifecycle. These are the little habits we miss but actually ground us in the past because they are so familiar.

7 WAYS FOR MASTERING FAILURE

The *psychological impact of failure* has a powerful influence on the way you live out your life. It influences the work you do, the people you hang out with, the decisions you make (or don't make), the opportunities you attract (or don't attract), and the quality of life experiences that you have.

Failure influences us in two ways:

1. **Failure is a great learning curve.** It's an educational experience, and you can implement your failings to do better the next time. Just as the salesperson keeps trying over and over to get that sale after hundreds of rejections, you turn failure into an ally, figure out an alternative approach, and pursue your goals relentlessly.
2. **Failing scares you.** At the very least, you are intimidated by the thought of failing. You play it safe and take small chances, too small to have any significant impact.

   Failure makes you question your self-worth, level of skill, and shakes your confidence so much that it could take you months to recover after one incident. Failure brings about stress and leverages fear so badly that you become depressed and feel totally worthless, helpless, and ashamed.

The Persuasive Power of Failing

Failure is very persuasive. It affects your happiness, self-esteem, and confidence. One enormous loss could set you back for months, years or decades. You might say, "I'd rather never face that trial again, so I'm playing it safe from now on." The psychological impact of failing causes us to retreat to safer ground.

Safety is a comfort zone that has its own dangers. You become weak when you close the door on future opportunities and rely on the stability of routine.

The Psychological Impact of Failure

Failing influences your life in many ways. Depending on the culture and environment you grow up in, the results can be devastatingly hard. You might try to please your parents, teachers, peers, your manager, or an institution that is deciding to hire you. Your life could hang in the balance if the person on the other end of the table is making a decision that could impact your future.

The fear is real and failing is real. But it is the courage you reveal by showing up to play the game that matters. For many years, I ran away from failure. And if I wasn't running from it, I was trying to create chaos that made my life fail with intention. This is what happens when your confidence, self-esteem and purpose are out of alignment. You feel so down about yourself that your attitude says, "Whatever happens, happens. Just get it over with."

This form of negativity influences the circumstances to turn against you. It breeds more failure and keeps the fear real

We all approach failing from either a negative or positive perspective. If I fail at something, it wasn't meant to be. If I succeed, I did something right. But win or lose, it doesn't matter. Stepping up to bat, knowing that the pitcher is one of the best in the world and your chances of striking out are 9/10, no matter the outcome, you showed up to play.

Failure is not the negative event we have made it out to be. It is just the reverse. Failure is your best friend, and the positive power it has is truly amazing. Failure will never lie or betray you. It is only deceptive when you try to pretend it doesn't exist. Failing your way through life is the surest way to winning. The hard way is the only way for high-performance champions.

Failure is your optimum growth tool. It is your weapon in the big game. It is not just the road to success, but it *is* the road you must be willing to take because most people refuse to do so.

7 Ways to Reduce Your Failure Rate

(1) Spend Quality Time with Successful Mentors

You are the average of the people you spend the most time with. This is why it is critical to spend quality time with the people supporting you and helping each other. This could be your team at work, family at home, or your close circle of friends. The people you spend quality time with empower you for success.

Your support team are the people who are there for you when you need them, and they need you. They don't let you give up or make excuses for not getting things done. They'll be there for you when life gets in the way and you need that extra push, a close talk, and the knowing they are there for you through the thick of it all.

Be observant of the people who are trying to hold you back. They may ask you, "Why are you doing this?" or "What's gotten into you?" We have to realize people are still struggling with their own demons and personal trials.

The people you spend time with is an investment, in your life and in theirs, too. Look around you at the five people you are with most of the time. Do you trust them? Can you talk openly and honestly with these people? Are they willing to go the distance with you in difficult times?

We all want that "dream team" of people who are there to support us Find a mentor or accountability partner whom you can lean on for support. A mentor can be there to guide you through rough times when you're struggling. Hire a life coach and have weekly sessions so you stay on track with your goals.

(2) Identify Your Achilles' Heel

In Greek mythology, Achilles was a Greek hero of the Trojan War. According to legend, Achilles—who was a powerful warrior and believed to be undefeatable—was killed after being shot in the heel by an arrow. Not even Achilles could have predicted this was how he was going to die. If Achilles had known beforehand this was his only vulnerable spot, he could have planned ahead to protect himself during the Trojan War. He was shot in the heel by an arrow and died.

We have areas in our lives in which we are not strong, and while it may not kill us—as it did Achilles—we could end up setting ourselves up for failure by not recognizing what that is.

In many situations when defeat is prominent, it is our inability to see what's coming that defeats us. It is this weak link that throws us off-balance. Not setting ourselves up for success before our biggest challenge is at hand can result in losing the battle before it begins.

You have a weak link that is setting you up for failure. You don't know what it is yet, but it's there. It sets us up for the fall and hits us when we least expect it. This could be a lack of awareness, a bad habit, an addiction not yet dealt with, or an old self-defeating belief.

Here are the top 9 "Achilles' Heels" people struggle to overcome. See if yours is on the list:

1. Overconfidence
2. Lack of Knowledge
3. Procrastination
4. Poor Health
5. Underestimating Your Opponent
6. Scattered Focus
7. Lack of Attention
8. Negative Mindset
9. Limited Thought Patterns

You won't always see defeat coming, but you can prevent it the best you can by taking these measures to reduce your chances of failing:

(3) Beat Your Achilles' Heel

1. Look back and make a note of the last three setbacks you have had. Do these setbacks have something in common?
2. what is the one area of your life in which you fail on a consistent basis? Is it your health? Relationships? The area of your life bringing you the most grief is telling you that there is a problem.
3. Make a list of the solutions you could start to work with. In the case of my procrastination habit, I made a list of tasks I had been putting off. I had things on my list dating back years. I was paying for it with guilt. Now, what can you do? What is the one small action you can take today?
4. Make this daily action a habit. Create a trigger, so you recognize when it is acting up.
5. Be sure to recognize the positive changes in your life by taking action. How do you feel emotionally? Are you more confident, at peace, or your mind is quitter than before?
6. Continue to focus on developing a system of continuous self-improvement. Don't let yourself fail.

Don't be caught off-guard. Be ready for when that day comes, and you know life is going to get the best of you. Fight back and get up when you get knocked down.

You will always have a weak link in your routine, habits, or way of thinking. Make a list of what these weak links are and keep working on eliminating them.

(4) Plan for the Future... Today

If you fail to plan in the present, you plan to fail in the future. Although I admit most of my thinking is centered in the present moment, I do have to plan for the future by taking care of business in the now.

For example, now is the time to eat healthy, not in twenty years when you're diagnosed with an illness. Now is the time to train and exercise, and not later when you're fifty pounds overweight.

Now is the time to plan for your financial future, and not five years before retirement. Now is the time to develop your relationships with your children, and not in ten years when they don't want to spend time with you anymore.

You should spend one hour a week reviewing your goals for the next year, month, week, and day. Time- block in one hour every Sunday afternoon or evening and drill down into your plans.

Are your projects up to date? Have you submitted the papers you filled out? Is there anything that came up this week you need to put into your planning funnel?

This hour could the most important hour of your week. If you want to do this right, I recommend you build this system into your routine. Make it a solid habit. Buy a yearly planner and a wall calendar. Make planning your week a solid commitment so that you are focusing in on the critical tasks that move you towards your goals.

Ask yourself:

- Who are you spending time with this week?
- What is your top 3 goals for the week/month?
- How much sleep do you want to get each night?
- What exercise are you going to do, when, and how long will each training session be?
- What would you like to learn today so you can grow your business by 10-20% over the next year?

"By failing to prepare, you are preparing to fail."

—Benjamin Franklin
Founding Father of the United States

(5) Ask for Help

One of the hardest things to do is ask for help. We are afraid of being rejected. If you don't ask, you don't get. And we need to elicit the help of others to get to where we want to be.

Think about all the things you are not asking for in your life. Chances are, you could fill up a page. Right now, take out a piece of paper and make a list of all the things you want to ask for, but have always been afraid to.

Here are some prompts to get you moving:

- "What am I afraid to ask my spouse for?"
- "What am I afraid to ask my best friend for?"
- "What am I afraid to ask total strangers for?"
- "What am I afraid to ask my mentor for?"
- "What am I afraid to ask my manager for?"
- "What am I afraid to ask myself for?"

Everyone has something they are afraid to ask for. Once you clearly identify the things you are afraid to ask for, you can move forward with the next phase:

"Why?"

Next to the list of things you are afraid to ask for, write down the reason why you are afraid to ask. This is the fuel that will move you into doing something about it. Knowing what you are afraid to ask for is the first step. It brings clarity to what you are hiding from. But the why should make you see how silly the fear is, and prompt you to push through it.

Here is my simple 6-step process for asking for what you want:

1. Write down—in a notebook or using the Evernote app—the one thing you really want.
2. Make a short list of three people who could provide this.
3. Write down the benefit you are providing by asking them for what you desire to have.
4. Ask confidently, as if it is already yours.
5. Be respectful of their decision if it doesn't turn out the way you wanted.
6. Finally, let go of your expectations.

You can make a massive difference in your life by asking the right people for the right things at the right time. Commit to asking for at least one thing you desire a day. This can be something you want for yourself, or better yet, to help someone else obtain something they want.

Visualize the one thing you asked for being given to you. That job you want, the loan, a promise, or a three- week vacation. Yes, anything is yours the moment you get the courage to ask for it. If you get refused? That is good. You now develop tougher skin for asking again.

(6) Consistently Improve by 1%

Where would you be one year from now if you focused on making small adjustments to your habits, thoughts, systems, or behavior by just 1%? Do you think this is a low % to shoot for? Why not be more ambitious and go for 20%?

Here is a strategy you can implement that contributes continuously towards your growth rate without creating an obstacle or feeling of overwhelm. If you've ever crammed for a test by trying to do all the studying the night before, you know what this feels like.

If you joined a marathon for the first time, would you start training several days before the event? This wouldn't be enough time. But, if you start training 4-6 months before and begin by running 1km a day, within two months, you will be conditioned to go the distance.

You can achieve most goals by applying the 1% rule. I often hear people say things like: "I have no time to read."

"If only I had an extra hour."

You only have to read for ten minutes a night. Read 3 pages if you can. If you don't have 30-60 minutes, invest the time you can when you can.

I can't get to the gym every night. So, it's tough to exercise at all. You don't need a gym. You can work out at home. In twenty minutes, you could do push-ups, pull-ups, or stretching. If you need to go to the gym, you go when you can, but when it's impossible, make it possible at home.

By doing the minimum, you are still working on the habit of showing up and not buying into your excuses of, "I can't because…"

You always can, even if it is just 1%.

(7) **ABP—Always Be Prepared**

I believe the single biggest reason people fail is from lack of planning. Failure always trails behind the person who is least prepared. If this is you, you're an easy target.

In order to reduce your rate of failing tomorrow, next week, and in the next decade, you want to prepare yourself by taking action today. Lack of action means lack of results.

I know someone who recently lost a relative. This relative was reasonably wealthy and when he passed away, he did so without a will. They had nothing to go by. No planning or discussion had taken place to prepare for this. In the end, the estate ended up in the hands of the state. Gone.

It pays to plan. Always. Always be prepared. I strongly encourage you to spend time every day, even if it is just for ten minutes, to look at the areas of your life where you are not ready for the unexpected. When the worst- case scenario comes raining down, will you be ready?

Make sure that you:

- Get health checks regularly. Don't wait until it is too late to do something about your health.
- Revise your financial plan. Do you want to work until you're 85 paying off debt? Start your financial plan today.
- Discuss the reality of dying with your family.
- Continue to learn new skills. You never know if you will show up at work one day and no longer have a job.
- Have a small, spare gas tank in the trunk with a spare tire. Take it from my experience, you don't want to be stranded in the middle of nowhere wishing you had filled up the gas tank yesterday.

Remember this: **If you don't have a plan for your future, rest assured, somebody else does.**

Failing Fast in Motion

- Figure out what you want.
- Identify obstacles and work on one at a time.
- Take a small step toward making your vision a reality.
- Ask the right people for help.
- Take time out to think about what you learned recently, and continue to improve on these lessons.
- Build this learning into your weekly planning
- ABP—Always Be Prepared.

THE 7-STEP FRAMEWORK FOR CONTINUOUS CHANGE

> *"I believe that one defines oneself by reinvention.*
> *To not be like your parents. To not be like your friends.*
> *To be yourself. To cut yourself out of stone."*
>
> —Henry Rollins

The process of growth is never a straight line to success. There isn't any magic formula for it. Change is what happens when you take implemental action toward the things that aren't working in your life. By cutting away and detaching from what is harming us (resentment, false fears, self-doubt) and replacing these with positive actions and developing a truer sense of who we are, you feel a stronger sense of self-actualization.

It is a reawakening of the parts of your life that have been dormant. That big piece of you that wasn't allowed to dream or feel, now suddenly wants to take a lead role in your life. We have to allow it that chance to grow and develop into what it wants.

I have made many changes in my life and have squared off against destructive behaviors that threatened to take everything away. But in this struggle, I learned the necessary elements one needs to win out. I have put the best of these steps in the rest of this free report.

Seven Steps to Continuous Change

1. Be responsible

The single biggest obstacle and fault that I see again and again with people who can't change is the inability to claim responsibility. We have talked about this already, but I'll mention it again because of its importance.

Without acknowledging our own role in this life, we'll struggle to feel responsible to do anything about it. Falling back on default behaviors will drive you back to the destructive, negative emotions of inferiority, shame, blame, and rejection. When this works against you, the victim mentality returns, and you become trapped again.

It adds to the frustration when you have to continually go back and restart everything. People give up because they get tired of the fight. While we can't avoid the struggle, we can make the journey less of an uphill battle by owning what we do.

As for change, in his bestselling book, *Awaken the Giant Within*, Tony Robbins said, "The belief that you and I must have if we're going to create long-term change is that we're **responsible for our own change**, not anyone else."

The world isn't going to change for you. Only you can change for yourself. By taking responsibility, and really owning it, we can rapidly speed up the process from years to days to hours. Change can happen as quickly as you want it to, but we must be ready to surrender.

2. Be willing to fail

We are afraid to take chances on ourselves because we might fail. But without failing at the things we love to do, we cannot move forward. And if you aren't moving forward, you're still stuck.

We covered the self-defeating failure mindset in chapter 7, but to reinforce it here, a willingness to make errors is healthy. Over the years, we developed a rebellious attitude toward the critics in our lives when we failed. They let us know that it isn't okay to be average. They reminded us that failure is the equivalent of "no good."

The journey isn't a straight line. There are holes on the road and we fall into these ruts all the time. But as they say, if you get knocked down, you can stay down or get back up again. Failing is nothing more than a lesson in life. It is a lesson that teaches resilience.

Those who accept their mistakes by realizing through self-actualization that it's okay to fall back at times will become stronger than those who shrink from the challenge. The key isn't just to keep going but, to make a firm commitment to never give up.

3. Practice self-compassion

We should be kind to ourselves above all else. Understand that you are doing everything you can now to make yourself a better person, someone who has more compassion and is capable of overcoming life's obstacles. Be good to yourself by engaging in fulfilling activities that add to self-esteem and self-love.

Here are some examples:

- Get plenty of rest.
- Spend time with someone talking about the journey you are both taking.
- Think about the many things you're grateful for in life.
- Stop trying to overachieve. Focus on self-development as your primary goal.

In addition to the above suggestions, I recommend that you have frequent review sessions with yourself. Take a look at the areas of your life that need the most work. Is it in your relationships with people? Are you physically out of shape? Do you suffer from negativity that keeps invading your thoughts?

Whatever it is, come up with several action steps you can implement to overcome the obstacle. For example, maybe you've been treating your body badly for many years by smoking, eating junk food, or drinking too much.

In order to reach that level of fulfillment in which you are happy with your physical self, you could get help to put an end to any addictive behavior you have. If you are overweight, you can start by eating better or joining a weight loss program.

These are all positive actions that build toward self-compassion. Reading this book, for example, is one way that you are contributing toward your new lifestyle. But reading a book doesn't mean anything if you can't put what you learn into action. To do this, you need to have regular "reflection sessions" in which you face the reality of where you are, who you are, and what you need to focus on to get to where you want to be.

Self-compassion involves tough self-love. You have to look at who you want to be, who you are now, and identify with what you don't like about yourself. We can only become the person we truly want to be by recognizing the person we are and the traits or habits that are damaging to us.

- This entails a disciplined course of action:
- Set up weekly sessions to review where you are.
- Identify the people you can reach out to for help.
- Do at least one activity a week that you enjoy, which brings you fulfillment.
- Stay resilient on the path that is committed to your continuous growth.

4. Engage in fulfilling relationships

The relationships in your life have a powerful impact on the change you succeed at. Someone in an abusive relationship will have a much better success rate at changing if they leave that relationship. If the people in your workplace are negative and holding you back, such as a critical boss or coworkers, leaving that job and searching for something else is a better option.

We need to decide with intention the type of relationships we want to have and invest in. If we are not clear about the kind of relationships we should be in, then we risk falling into the relationships that damage, hurt, and destroy our self-esteem.

Intimate relationships with people who foster our growth form a mutual relationship of respect and love. I have seen massive growth in people after they broke away and ended relationships that were damaging their lives.

Are you in a situation in which someone is extremely critical of you? Do they hold you back from moving ahead because they are afraid you might change and leave them behind? Do you struggle to communicate with these people because they refuse to listen to ideas you have about building a better life?

We need to dive deep and analyze the relationships we're in now, and also the relationships we have a habit of forming.

5. Focus on self-esteem building strategies

Self-esteem is like a wave of growth. Some days it is up, but on those days when things aren't going so well, it can drop, bringing with it your confidence and positive thoughts. But if you have self-esteem strategies built in to counterattack this when it happens, you'll be in a better position to raise your energy levels any time you want. Then, instead of relying on your feelings to control how you are handling things, you can put these strategies into play whenever you want.

Self-esteem strategy #1: Focus on small, achievable tasks. You can build your self-esteem by being successful at accomplishing small projects instead of trying to take on too much. Focus on what is realistic and follow a step-by-step approach. In other words, easy does it.

Self-Esteem Strategy #2: Learn a new skill. Is there something you've always wanted to learn but you lacked the commitment or confidence to pursue it? Skill-building is a powerful way to increase self-esteem. It also supports change and is a positive-building activity.

Self-Esteem Strategy #3: Be aware of the way you speak to yourself. Our mind has a way of returning back to the negative state it is accustomed to. When you start to beat up on yourself, switch it around and use positive affirmations and self-affirming thoughts. Don't allow yourself to tear down all the work you have put in.

6. Hire a life coach

I strongly encourage you to hire a life coach or find a mentor for your journey. This makes a massive difference in recovering from the condition of negative patterns. Being able to reach out and talk to someone you trust is the best solution. But how do you find a mentor? Where are these people?

Define the qualities you are looking for in a life coach or a mentor. Who is in the best position to help you? Is there someone you know personally who could mentor you? If not, could you join a help group or connect with someone who is going through a similar experience?

Make a list of traits your ideal mentor has. Why are these traits important to you?

For example, your mentor is someone who…

- Listens carefully with passion and concern, offering suggestions when needed.
- Relates to their partner's world through sharing similar experiences.
- Teaches through showing, not just telling.
- Challenges their partner to find ways to solve problems and help themselves.
- Helps their partner discover their own solutions to real life-problems but doesn't take on the burden of solving their problems.
- Walks together with you on the journey, side-by- side, while you hold each other up should the other person fall.
- Teaches through perseverance and patience.
- Sets people up for success, nurturing them along the way

and giving them space to grow, but is always ready to share the burden when it becomes too heavy.
- Is committed to the growth, expansion, development, and spiritual well-being of the people they mentor.
- Shares their vision, dreams, and desires with their mentoring partners, while helping them to achieve their own dreams through the pursuit of excellence.

7. Learn Skills to Increase Influence

One of the fastest paths to creating change is learning a new skill that influences your rapid growth cycle. Rapid growth is the result of applying what you learn to generate a result. As Tom Bilyeu of **Impact Theory** states: "Skills build utility."

So, what does this mean? It means that, regardless of your education, background, or past achievements, you can always learn new skills that build towards something you really want. Change is the result of taking intentional action that moves you in the direction of something that you're passionate about and brings fulfillment into your life.

8. Make Change a Continuous Cycle

This requires daily work, but you can do it by staying focused on moving forward and taking small actions on a consistent basis. We have books we can read, courses we can take, and a ton of resources available at our fingertips.

Be clear about your goals and the habits you want to develop. This is a good chance to focus on the habits and behaviors holding you back.

CONTROL DISTRACTIONS AND MANAGE SHINY OBJECT SYNDROME

You are in a constant struggle to maintain control of your mind. One minute, you are working on your #1 priority. The next minute, you are watching a cat video.

And you don't even like cats.

In the beginning, when I became aware of my addiction to distraction, I created a habit to mark down how often I had a thought to go do something else. To give you an example, I'm writing an article for this week's newsletter. It has to be done end of day because I send it out every Tuesday. It normally takes 2-3 hours to write this article, but before I started tracking my distractions, one article took me three days to complete. Three days! Why?

Attention Disorder. Another term to describe this is *Monkey Mind*. It is a Buddhist term meaning unsettled, restless, capricious, whimsical, fanciful, inconstant, confused, indecisive, and uncontrollable. In other words, a *Monkey Mind* is highly prone to becoming distracted by anything and everything.

I call this chasing rabbit trails. It's also a symptom of *Shiny Object Syndrome* (SOS).

Shiny Object Syndrome trains your mind to seek out a shiny object that distracts your attention. This could be a course, information, another book, or a social media ad. Meanwhile, as you pursue these things, you leave behind a trail of broken objects (aka unfinished tasks). As we looked at earlier, completing your open loops must be your priority. You have to finish it. If it's an ongoing project, you must complete the one task within that project.

But what do I do if I suddenly catch myself running down another path? You STOP. Take a STEP BACK. BREATH.

Task switching wears you down fast. Can you imagine what you'll accomplish with one hour of focused work on a specific task for the next **30** days?

I can tell you what would happen. You'd finish that one thing you're focused on. There is no great mystery to unlock here. Most of your issues with procrastination stem from the impulse to run in a different direction to the course you *should* be taking.

You're always in pursuit of the next best thing. You jump from idea to idea without clarity on what you need or want. You end up wasting time, money and resources.

Eventually, Shiny Object Syndrome (SOS) wears you down. The only thing worse than not having the right information or tools for the job is having too much information and too many tools.

When you show up to build a house, you don't need five different hammers. Only one good hammer will do!

SOS is a condition of the mind. It continues to win over your mind until you make that conscious effort to retrain your brain. The negative effects of SOS are:

Inability to finish projects. When you get excited about a new project before your first one is complete, you may jump ship before you can see any meaningful results.

Poorly planning your ideas and directives. People with SOS tend to focus on the thrill of pursuing a given strategy, or making a specific change, rather than the strategy or change itself.

For example, they may love the idea of creating a new product and begin work on developing it but have no long-term game plan on how to follow through on that idea. This leads to poor results from an underdeveloped execution and unrealized potential.

Spending lots of cash. There are hundreds of technological tools for businesses that are impressive, effective and fun to use. Unfortunately, if you subscribe to all these services, or you jump from platform to platform, you'll end up burning through so much cash that they become incredibly cost-inefficient. As a result, you'll have less money available to invest in your business.

I've spent thousands of dollars chasing plenty of objects. Why? I was looking for something to give me the clarity I needed. I was able to correct this with a few simple steps in my habits and thought process.

Here's what you can do to gain control of your mind: Limit Your choices

Marketers these days are savvy in their approach to presenting everything as an urgent "must-have". Why do you need **10** books on productivity if you have **1-2** of the best books? Do you need 3 different subscriptions to software when one does everything you want/require?

Getting lost in the weeds, we forget to focus on the fruits of our garden. SOS is watering the weeds and not the crops that matter.

Distraction isn't the external issue. You don't control distraction by controlling all the things fighting for your attention. You simply focus on the one thing that needs your attention NOW. Limit your choice preference and choose.

Distraction is a focus issue and not a result of having too many things to pursue. If you have ten rabbits running around in your field, you decide on the one to pursue.

I bought into the Shiny Object Syndrome for years. I would buy this and that, try this service and that one. I was convinced that if I just bought the next perfect service, I could eventually stop pursuing everything.

Then a new one would crop up.

The challenge with SOS is that you are always looking for the next better option. And there is always a better option than the one you just bought.

Before you click that buy button, talk about it with someone at home or on your team. Do you need this tool, training course or service? If so, map out the benefits it provides to your life and business.

Chances are, given time to consider, you'll realize you don't actually need it. Not only that but, in a few weeks, you'll see another similar product or service that almost does the same thing, but it actually is better and cheaper.

Don't believe them when they say, "You have ten minutes to grab this at 30% off." It's a marketing tactic, and it works. But if you dial into the same service or product next week, guess what, you'll hear the same story.

Compare the products on offer. When I shop online, I compare prices to this and that. After comparing prices, I can usually find it for cheaper. Impulsive shopping could cost you hundreds or thousands of dollars a year.

Work on one thing at a time. If you are immersed in one project now, you don't need something else that is out of alignment with what you are presently focused on. I know what it's like to be ambitious and biting off more than I can chew.

Finish your project and, if you decide later this "shiny thing" is the best tool or option, grab it. Chances are, by the time you have completed your one thing, you will have forgotten all about it.

Review your goals. Check your goals for the month and the quarter. If you don't have your goals written down, check out my book, *Empower Your Big Goals*, and work on this. Reviewing your goals will bring everything into alignment. If the shiny object isn't related to what you're working on right now, leave it alone.

This is where many people fail. "But I can get it now and use it later!" You probably won't use it later, and anyway, won't it be available in three months when you need it? Probably. It can wait, and so can you.

The bottom line is, Shiny Object Syndrome leads to distraction procrastination. It deepens your procrastination habit, and we want to unwind it, not strengthen it. Once you recognize this condition, you can correct it. I didn't realize I had SOS until I looked at all the stuff I'd bought and the courses I signed up for. Once I woke up to my SOS, it changed everything.

Before I begin the chase, I do this:

Stop. Don't do anything.

Think about it.

Argue the pros and cons with someone you trust.

STay as you are for 24 hours

RevIsit the decision/discussion in 48 hours.

Complete what I'm doing first.

I call this the **STATIC** method. When you find yourself overwhelmed with too many choices, or confusion is making it difficult to concentrate, remember the STATIC steps and slow it down.

Don't make any impulsive decisions. Stop and think it through. If you feel rushed or you experience a rush from buying into something you're not 100% on, do nothing. Wait. Breathe. Take your time. Massive action doesn't mean jumping at everything you see.

You'll be able to serve your business and sanity by giving up pursuing those shiny objects. In forty-eight hours, you could feel completely different and glad you had taken the time to reflect.

Less is always more. You want the most efficient and cost-effective tools and services, not a massive abundance of various tools all doing the similar function.

Implementation Task:

Now that you know what SOS is and how to manage the syndrome, build awareness into the temptation to pursue it. Use the **STATIC** strategy.

Sit on ideas before launching them. Before you begin work on the new project that's going to "change everything," take a moment. Wait until tomorrow. Delay the impulse to buy or start something new.

Finish building your bridge. There is a saying about half-built bridges. You can't reach the other side. This is true for your goals and workflow.

Imagine a company that builds products, and instead of finishing one and launching it, they start building a new product. Nothing gets completed, and that company goes bankrupt. Finish what you're doing. Work on one thing at a time. Complete the project before moving to the next.

Reduce your research time. Stop looking for new things. If you have the information you need, why get more? If you have the course or book or manual to do your work, do you need more? Probably not. Shiny objects give us a sense of euphoria in getting something new. It's like buying a new car. And after a few weeks you're looking to trade it in for a better model. Stick with what you have.

7 WAYS TO RETRAIN YOUR BRAIN

"In order to carry a positive action, we must develop here a positive vision."

—Dalai Lama

Our thoughts have a direct influence on the way we live. Our quality of life can be traced back to the quality of our own thoughts. But how often do you find yourself trapped in a negative thought-loop that just spins on forever? How much mental energy is spent on replaying the old tapes from your past and listening to the critical voices that feel like they are running the show?

Eliminate Negative Thinking and Take Control of Your Thoughts

Just as a positive mindset fills you up with creative energy, your negative mindset, and the negative thoughts that go with it, deplete your mental and physical energy. You feel lethargic. You get headaches more frequently. You are less motivated to work, play, or interact with anyone.

The core of your focus is on what you don't like, who you resent, what you don't have, and how bad life has turned out for you. Negative thinking is poison for your mind.

Your mission: Eliminate this noise

But it isn't just your mind that is affected. Your physiology is influenced, as well. Negative thoughts make you sick more often, and because you think you are depressed, you take medication. Only instead of helping you to overcome the real core issues, you stay depressed and continue to live in a world of negativity.

In most cases, it is not our environment that needs to change. It isn't the other people that have to shape up and treat you better. You don't have to hope for things to get better, because they won't. You *make* things better by deciding to transform your thoughts.

Negative thoughts—just like positive ones—don't happen by pure chance. We create our own misery, just the same as we create our own happiness. Surprisingly, many people believe that happiness is what happens when things work out perfectly, or when we finally get everything we want in life.

Until then, we stay neutral or miserable, struggling through our days, hoping for the best. Negative thoughts thrive in this environment. Your negative persona is searching for a reason to exist. When you focus on what you don't have, how bad the economy is, or the bad situation you are in, you open the door for your negative thoughts to take over.

Here is what S.J. Scott says about negative thoughts, from his book *Declutter Your Mind* with Barrie Davenport:

> *"Many people go through their entire lives victimized by their negative thoughts. They feel they have no control of what thoughts take up residence in their brains—and worse, they believe the 'voices' in their heads that tell them the sky is falling."*

Though it may feel natural to allow your mind to wander into worry and despair, you're reinforcing negative thinking by not challenging it and by accepting your thoughts as your identity. But you have the power to recognize this tendency and change it by building the reframing habit.

From now on, I want you to picture negative thoughts as intruders, taking up space in your head. If they stay there, you will continue to repeat past failures. Knock each of these intruders out of your mind as they pop up.

If you don't do this, you will fail to achieve your goals and every action you take will feel like an uphill battle. Negative thinking is powerful but remember: You are responsible for feeding into it. You create your own thoughts—good or bad.

What happens when we build negative thoughts into our thought paradigm? The world becomes a dark, painful existence. For me, suffering is when I let the demons of negativity take over and run my emotions.

When you are stuck in a negative frame of mind, and you think there is no way out, you will stop looking for the exit. I don't know of anyone who purposefully *wants* to suffer.

Yet, our negative thinking is just that: a form of self-destruction. For many people, we go through days—and even weeks—in which things are not going right. Negative thoughts can be triggered by a crisis in your family, a trauma at work, a painful breakup, or financial burden. Life is not fair, but then again, what *is* fair? When everything works out perfectly, and we get everything we want without having to work for it?

"Life isn't fair." This is a statement to the universe that says, "I am a victim in this life, and I deserve better." The people who deserve better are the people who *make it better*. Sitting around, waiting for change, is the same as expecting to win the lottery when you don't even buy lottery tickets.

Let's look at how you can retrain your brain to think differently. You are never too old, too educated, or too good for leveling up your mind and ridding yourself of the negative influences that have planted their flag in your mind.

Picture this as a new garden that you worked hard to plant and grow your seeds. The next day, the garden is corrupted by weeds. Would you walk away and let them grow, destroying all your work? Of course not.

As **James Allen** said:

> *"A person sooner or later discovers that he or she is the master-gardener of their soul, the director of his or her own life."*

You are the master-gardener, and this is your life. It doesn't obey circumstances, and you are not stuck doing anything you don't want to do. Your thoughts—and the actions you take that are driven by thought—build your tomorrow. You will always follow through on what your mind is telling you to do. But who is giving the commands?

You are

Let's look at how you and I are influenced by the random thoughts that just pop up and start ruining everything. Most of your thoughts are so normal (to you) that you likely don't even question them. But these are the areas of our thinking we need to pay attention to the most. It is what we accept as "natural" that is the hardest to change because we can't always see it.

Sometime others may be point it out. They might say, "Hey, you are really rude sometimes," or worse. But if we fail to even recognize it, we will refute the claim and continue to act like a jerk. Imagine if you could alter just one pathway in your mind. What could you achieve?

After all, this is what mental roadblocks are: obstacles that stick because we don't have the tools to remove them.

But we do now. You have this book, and the corresponding material to go with it, so change it, you can—and you will! Nothing is impossible—unless your thoughts tell you it is. But that doesn't make it true.

Now, let's dive into the strategies for retraining your brain to recognize your negative thoughts and free your mental blocks. Then, you will know a freedom like nothing else.

The Danger of Negative Thinking

We know negative thinking is not healthy. It's not like we wake up every morning and decide to make it the worst day we've ever had. But that is what happens to millions of people every day. They move through life, listening to the toxic voices inside, believing the criticisms and fearful thoughts provoking us to worry and feel anxious.

Where do you think worry comes from? Worry is a result of being fearful of the future. Anxiety has a strong part to play in your past. You know you can't change anything from what has been said and done, so you linger back there, trying to sort out what happened, replaying angry conversations, and hanging on to old resentments.

Our thoughts are dangerous if we let them run loose. We end up sabotaging what could be glorious moments and destroying memories in a moment. Think about this: **Your emotions will always follow your thoughts.**

Imagine going through life angry. Every day, you are pissed-off, fearful, and frightened. Now, take it a step further. Because you're always angry, you take it out on your family or a pet. When they do something that annoys you, how do you react? In anger. Your negative, angry thoughts are not only damaging your own mind.

You can exercise that power in the world by bringing it out into the open. Soon the people who are around you disappear. They remember you as that person who was always in a bad mood. What creates a mood? The thoughts you have been dwelling on all week.

Recognize your negative thoughts, change them day by day, and gradually your life becomes a better memory. You will draw people to you instead of scaring them away. Remember that your external reality will always reflect your internal thought processes. What you think about all day long is who you become.

It is such an easy concept. People think they need to figure everything out and get to the root of the problem. So, what do they do? They expect the other person to change so they can feel better. Haven't you ever said to yourself: "I wouldn't feel this way if he would just…."

The world and the people in it do not owe you anything. Nobody will recognize that they are in the wrong even if you point it out to them. It is up to you to find meaning in your own thinking patterns and look to change it. And by change it I mean, transform your thoughts. I know, easier said than done, right? But not impossible. People change every day. It may take months to see results, but it starts now.

To recap, negative thinking does the following:

- Sabotages your future;
- Destroys potentially good memories;
- Ruins your physical and mental health;
- Creates anger that sabotages relationships;
- Increases the chances of depression;
- Makes us restless and irritable; and
- Creates feelings of desperation.

Remove Negative Phrases That Keep You Stuck

How many negative phrases can you count in a day? I'll bet you have as many as I do, and I can catch myself on many of them. But what makes these negative connotations stick is that we justify being used or abused.

- "If only he/she would stop…."
- "I can't believe they did that. Now I'm screwed."
- "Nothing ever works out for me. I told you so."
- "He makes me so angry."
- "Everything would be so perfect if only…."
- "All I want is (fill in your desire here) and then I'll be happy."
- "See how much she has, and look at how little I have?"
- "Life just isn't fair."
- "Some people have all the luck."

By playing the victim, you place yourself in a position of power. You want to be right and they are wrong. You want to be understood while the misunderstanding lies with the other person. You want an apology for being wronged so you can justify how right you always are.

Here is what I do. Carry a small notebook with you. You can use a tablet, but I prefer actual paper because digital material gets lost easily. Throughout the day, when you start to complain or use one of your negative phrases, write it down. Right there. This will make you aware of what you are thinking and saying that keeps your self-pity train moving.

Self-pity is another form of negative thought. It spins a web of lies that tell us, "If I am the victim, I don't have to do anything." Use your notebook to identify the phrases you use. Then, add up the phrases you have most commonly used. Everybody has several that they love to use repeatedly.

Disempower Your Inner Voice

We all have a big, loud inner voice. You can hear this voice clearly when you try something new, when you fail, or when you are feeling afraid. It is the voice of self- sabotage, and it is not too kind. This voice is your mind is feeding you lies, and it always has. It is strong because you have listened to it for so long, it sounds normal.

To quiet this voice, you must replace it with another voice—your true voice. This is the voice of compassion. It is the voice you were born with and not the tormented demon that runs lose inside your head, trying to create havoc.

When your thoughts are in such a disorganized array, it

seems you have little to no control over them. But that isn't true. You can stop the roller coaster of disempowering thoughts anytime. You have the power to throw the switch and put an end to your inner critic. It may take a lot of attempts but, every time it speaks up, shut it down.

Recognize Who and What Triggers Negative Thoughts.

Most of your negative thinking is attached to something—a person, place or situation—that acts as a trigger. If it is a person, they could be your spouse, neighbor, or co-worker/manager. Sometimes, all it takes is one thought about this person to send you on a negative tangent in your mind that could derail your entire day.

By focusing on the object of your anger and resentment, you are feeding the negative energy that keeps it alive. You can blame, criticize, and condemn as much as you like, but the only one that suffers is yourself.

> *"Your mind is the basis of everything you experience and of every contribution you make to the lives of others. Given this fact, it makes sense to train it."*
>
> —Sam Harris

I know one man who was fired from his job over a misunderstanding with his employer. For months, he was angry. When he drove past the building the company was located in, he became hostile and violent and developed a deep resentment. What was triggering this? He was deliberately driving past the building and setting off his negative energy.

Once he recognized this trigger and quit this destructive

habit, the negative thoughts were gradually replaced with a better outlook that focused on getting a better job.

You could be hung up on a breakup, harboring a resentment toward your parents, or focusing on ways to get back at someone for injuring you emotionally or financially. Triggers set us up for failure and drag us into the depths of negative bias. We can conjure up all sorts of reasons to hold onto our resentments. But the only thing we will succeed at doing is feeding into our own misery.

Take note of what your trigger is, whether it is a person or place, and start removing these thoughts from your mind.

Here is one idea: Try the rubber-band trick. Place 5-10 rubber bands on your wrist. When you get stuck on a negative thought, take one of the bands and move it to your other wrist. This is a great visual aid to show you just how many negative thoughts you have, and how much progress you are making to crush those thoughts.

Stay Engaged with Positive Action

Staying engaged in a project or a hobby that you are passion about keeps negative thinking out of your head. It is hard to let bad thoughts grow when you are happy and working on something that has meaning to you.

Examples of this are:

- Studying another language
- Learning to play a musical instrument
- Listening to inspiring music
- Writing a book
- Creating a business plan

- Working on repairs for your house
- Reading a book
- Working on your goals

Taking positive action is the best way to stay engaged and when your mind is occupied with a creative activity, negative thinking has less chance of occupying your mental space.

Identify Your Common Worries

Everyone worries about something. In fact, it is nearly impossible to remove the habit of worrying. The best you can do is reduce the amount of time you spend worrying.

Do you know which area of your life you worry about the most? We all have things that cause us stress, and when this happens, our thoughts latch onto the uncertainty of the future. Do you worry about:

- Having enough money for retirement;
- Your child's future;
- Someone's plans to build a high-rise in your quiet neighborhood
- The next election?

While most of our worries are fleeting and last just a few minutes, it is your chronic, repetitive worries you want to zero in on. How many times a day do worrisome thoughts cross your mind about lack of money? Does this keep you awake late at night? Do you feel short of breath or panicked if you think about how little you have? Does this cause you to react aggressively?

Worry is a form of habitual thinking that sets us up for

failure. You can't be caught up in thoughts of worry and have a peaceful mind at the same time. The way to eliminate the chronic worry habit is to act on the thing that worries you.

Are you afraid of not having money? Get educated on financial planning and set up a savings plan.

Kids' future? Talk with your kids about what they want to do. But remember: You are worrying about something you have no control over. Worrying about the future is pointless. It is a gray zone in which anything can happen.

Stay centered in the present moment and worrisome thoughts will not follow you there.

Put an End to Labeling

How many times a day do you label things as good, bad, or ugly? Here are some examples:

- "She's a real…"
- "I can't stand that guy. He's such a…"

You know how it goes. We condemn, judge, and assassinate the character of other people. We've all done it. Some people do it every day. For others, it is a habit that destroys their mindset. Yes, labeling is the #1 most destructive form of negativity you can practice. You tear down the reputation of others, while falsely building your own.

If you want to be free of negativity, the labeling must end. I don't mean just cut it in half—*get rid of it*.

But what about when someone makes me angry? Or insults me? Or they do something like rip me off or cut me off in traffic?

You're right. People act in disrespectful, arrogant, malicious ways all the time. Welcome to the real world. Not everybody plays nice. But will you throw away your mental toughness by lowering yourself to the act of labeling.

Calling someone out on their actions is a better way to approach this than labeling them for an action they have taken. Remember that peoples' behavior doesn't always reflect their true character. People make mistakes, do things out of character, and react toward a situation based on their experiences.

5 STEPS TO LEVERAGING FEAR (AND BECOMING YOUR BEST)

We all want a better way to handle our fear and to live a fearless lifestyle. We all want better strategies for confronting the people, places and things that challenge our confidence. Better yet, we want to take action when it is called for so we can become fearlessly confident and succeed in the areas of life that matter

The intentional action you take today decides the level of fear you have to live with. Fear is not that complex. It just looks that way when you are faced with a fearful situation and you don't have an effective or immediate solution that works.

We feel afraid when our comfort zone is challenged. We feel afraid when we have a problem and lack the means to deal with it. We are afraid when our financial security is at risk. We may become terrified when failure is the necessary step to success.

This is why I have created a simple 5-step solution to living life to the max and becoming great in everything you do.

If you are ready...

Action Step #1: Know your fear

We all have our areas of life where fear is the greatest. It could be at work, at home, social anxiety or personal challenges. You can take a moment to identify with what scares you the most right now.

Is there something you are procrastinating on doing? Do you avoid certain situations because you might be rejected? In what situations do you experience fear the most?

By knowing how fear is impacting you in a specific area, this is where you can focus your energy to fight back. Identify the areas in your life where fear is controlling you. Do you fear losing something or someone? Is it the fear of taking on a new role that you might fail at? We can know our fear by understanding what drives it.

Action Step #2: Let go of past mistakes and future expectations

Fear exists in two states: the past and the future. We are trapped in past memories of things we failed at. The past has all our dirty little secrets [come on, you have at least one].

The future holds everything we are afraid of happening [and most of it doesn't happen]. If your mind is stuck in one place or the other, you will create a fearful state for yourself.

Staying in the present, focusing on what you can do today, is the best use of your time and energy. After All, your future is happening right now. The past is the result of how you are choosing to live right now. Both your past and future are the conditions created and being created in the now.

We hold onto our past because we are obsessed with what we could have done differently. Should I have chosen door 2 instead of door 3? Did I make the right decision? I approach this thinking with a simple affirmation: *I let go of my regrets.*

I am grateful for lessons that my past missteps have taught me.

The future is a fearful place full of our expectations. Will I get what I want? Will I fail and lose everything? What if…?

I handle this wildly spinning train of thought with a simple affirmation: *I have every quality I need to become hugely successful in all future endeavors.*

Recommended read: Eckhart Tolle discusses this topic at great length in his inspiring book The Power of Now.

Action #3: Remind yourself this is going to end someday

Life is short. We have just enough time to have a few laughs, cry a little, do important work that has an impact, and be the best we can be. This all takes place in about seventy years, give or take.

Every day you spend worrying, you create anxiety that reinforces your fearful state. Remember: you have a limited amount of time here. For some, they have less than others. It will all end someday and the only thing that is going to matter are the people you loved and the experiences you created.

Are you sharing the best of yourself with the people you care most about? Are you helping out somebody without any expectation in return?

When you are gone, you will be remembered for what you gave to the world, and not what you could collect or how much you owned.

Action #4: Spend twenty minutes a day focusing on being in the present moment

There is nothing more calming than the present moment. This

is one big reason why millions of people have taken to activities like meditation and yoga.

Spend time with yourself just sitting, deep thinking, and focusing on your breathing. Your fears will have no space in your mind when you control the direction of your thoughts.

Fearful thoughts and feelings take over when our attention is multi-divided. We can work ourselves into a state of panic and frustration. You could lose sleep or get physically sick. The present moment is the only state of time we have.

Take twenty minutes out of your day to get grounded. You should do this several times a day. Block that time in and make it a ritual.

Spend time:

1. Meditating.
2. Visualizing succeeding at your goals.
3. Listening to music that inspires you to take action
4. Observing your thoughts and turning your negative thoughts into positive.

Action #5: Don't waste your life

This seems like an obvious statement. But make the most of your time. Watch less TV. Play less video games. Turn off social media for a day.

Spend more time reading, talking to people about topics that make a difference, and take long walks in nature. Build quality activities into your daily routine.

People who walk around filled with fear are trapped in an existence of suffering. You can suffer less by being present and taking positive actions towards making your life amazing.

Do you want to live an amazing life or a fearful one?

Fear is a powerful motivator. It is a signal board that communicates with each of us. *Whatever it is you are afraid of, that is an area of your life that needs attention.*

If you have a fear of being alone, it is because you desire to be with others but are afraid of the risk of rejection. A fear of money or not having money signals that you have to create a better financial plan for yourself. If you are afraid of getting sick, you could eat better and start exercising. **Take action** towards whatever worries you have. Worry is not a positive action. It creates stress and negativity.

Look at fear as a companion on your journey. It communicates what you should be looking at. Recognize the fears that are holding you back.

What can you do?

What I did is create a fear journal. I made a list of the things that scared me, and the actions I was avoiding. They ranged from poor financial planning to filling out application forms to communicating with people I didn't want to talk with.

Then, for each week, I'd focus on one of these pain points. By doing something, not only did I remove that fear but, I had built up fearless confidence to deal with it.

Excessive worry, anxiety and all the other dysfunctions that come with it destroy your peace of mind. But taking action and doing something about it is the way of the fearless warrior.

You can leverage fear to become great at anything in your life.

What is holding you back? What do you fear today that you could take intentional action towards from today?

Now is the time to create your **fearless action list** and **get to work.**

7 TIPS FOR HANDLING REJECTION SENSITIVITY

One of the greatest illusions about rejection is that we convince ourselves we are being personally "rejected," as if someone is doing something to us. But in fact, the rejection begins on the inside. This can be traced back to your inner critics, those old voices that tell you, "You're no good," or "Why bother? You'll just fail anyway."

When we reject ourselves first, we are sending a clear message to people. It is like putting the writing on the wall yourself. People can sense when someone is lacking confidence. If you walk into a bank to get a loan and you believe—even before you meet with the loans officer—that there's no way you'll get the loan, this feeling carries with you. Be aware of situations in which you're rejecting yourself before anyone else gets a chance to.

Stop blaming external forces for failed results

Taking full responsibility for your life and current situation is a powerful character-building step. By taking charge, you take control. Deciding to stop blaming others for your unhappiness is taking a healthy approach to being responsible. This doesn't mean you have to forget what happened in the past, but you do have to move on from it.

This can only happen when you choose to live life on your terms by making a firm decision and following through with action to create a positive and fulfilling future. You are giving yourself permission to be free. Nobody else will give that to you. Once you accept your life as it is and are willing to do whatever it takes to move forward, then you are ready to be responsible.

Practice forgiveness, acceptance, and commit to moving forward. Don't stay stuck in one spot, waiting for someone else to make it all better. When you wait for someone else to take charge, you lose the chance to make the situation better and the opportunity to heal yourself is gone.

Take an opinion as a biased lack of knowledge

Everyone has an opinion. It is one of the ways we communicate our thoughts and emotions. We formulate opinions about each other based on what is said, actions taken, or differences in personality. If you struggle with rejection, then varying opinions can have a negative impact on your confidence.

We take the opinions and judgments from others as a personal insult. If someone doesn't like the way you look or dress, or they don't like your attitude and the way you carry yourself, you may take this too personally. There are many details other people use to construct an opinion about you as a person.

It is easy to believe everything you hear, especially if you are hypersensitive. Even though we can't stop the world from having opinions, we can choose how to accept it. Will you retaliate and come back with your own attack? Or will you take what is said as a biased remark based on lack of evidence? Besides, who really knows you better than yourself? Why should you take someone else's word as the only truth when you know it just isn't so?

This works the other way, too. Your evaluation of another person is based on the same lack of information that others use to construct their opinions about you. You have two choices here: You can continue the negative cycle of labeling others just as they label you, or you can practice total acceptance as a strategy to build more empathy toward others.

A lack of empathy is at the core of many social problems. When we buy in to the opinions and criticisms of strangers, we believe what *they* decide is the truth about us. But it's not. Rarely are first opinions correct.

Revisit your shame-based childhood.

For most people, living in rejection has its roots in early childhood. Back then, we were treated without the attention or respect we deserved. Criticism was rampant. We were never good enough, no matter how hard we tried or what level of success we could achieve. This resulted in a life of living in shame, a core attribute of those who feel rejected.

It can be a painful experience to revisit this period of our lives when not everything was perfect. But by returning to that particular event in your past when you were most vulnerable, and by walking yourself through that pain again, in time you can mend the damage that was inflicted.

Let go of the past failures that define you

If you were rejected in the past, you'll reject yourself in the future. We replay old stories of failures and negative results from our past. When this happens, we create more of the same. Your past is not who you are; it is who you were. Are you the same person you were twenty years ago? I know I'm not.

Sure, many things about you haven't changed and people still refer to you as someone they know based on a lifetime of friendship. But we are all evolving even if those changes are subtle. Basing your future happiness or success on what you got in the past is a way to repeat history. You can define your future by the actions you take now. Your thoughts, words, and emotions are powerful and can change your life in a moment if conditioned properly.

Practice getting rejected on purpose

In his bestselling book, *Rejection Proof*, Jia Jiang takes on a massive challenge. He set out to get rejected over the course of 100 days in a project he dubbed 100 Days of Rejection.

During this social experiment, Jia would try outrageous stunts of courage to push his fear of rejection beyond anything he had ever experienced. He would ask for Olympic symbol donuts, give $5 to five random people, and challenge a CEO to a staring contest. His purpose was to desensitize himself to rejection so that he could overcome his fears in order to live his dream as an entrepreneur.

So, how about you? In what ways could you put yourself out there and get rejected in order to numb yourself to the fear? We put more effort into avoiding fear than encouraging it. So when rejection happens (and it will) it hurts and we remember the pain as something we'd rather not repeat. As a result, we stay away from it as much as possible.

Build your confidence through consistent practice

The way to build confidence is to take action. Challenge yourself to do the things that are difficult. These are easy to spot because we resist what we don't want to do. Or we put off difficult tasks because they are hard but actually carry the greatest rewards in the long run.

Confidence is an "action building" activity. It can only be built when we put our fears and uncertainties to the test. You can use this list of Rejection Strategies as a starting point to develop a higher level of confidence and assurance.

Be Good to Yourself

One of the biggest hang-ups that defeat many people is the habit of beating up on themselves. They continuously repeat negative thoughts to themselves like "I am not worthy of love," "I am no good," or "I have nothing of value to give to anyone."

They do this through reinforcing conditional behaviors that defeat their actions. By beating themselves up through negative self-talk and harsh criticism, they minimize their personal value by buying into the "I'm worthless" mindset.

This is the great lie that perpetuates itself and grows stronger over the years. The more we repeat these negative messages to ourselves, the more real they become. This has to end if we are to expand beyond our current state.

What I want you to do is give yourself a break here. You are not perfect, but by reading this book you have taken a positive step by making a clear decision to improve yourself.

You could be hard on yourself because somebody else was hard on you. It is time to step up and start being good to yourself. Later on, I will show you the strategies for dealing with nasty negatives. You'll learn how to turn words of self-defeat and limited thoughts into empowering positives that create long-term growth and change.

Observe Your Reactions

Starting today, observe how you react to challenging situations. How do you feel around people you think are better than you? What thoughts are going through your mind that devalues your self-worth? When do you feel irritated? Angry? Fearful? Rejected?

This observation is an important step. For now, you don't have to figure anything out. Just watch how you react. You will start to see a pattern develop that you have not noticed before.

Reactions are conditioned behaviors that take the place of common sense and wisdom. By starting to notice your reactions now, you can develop better ways to handle situations that used to baffle you.

Overreacting, or reacting out of fear, is a coping strategy when we feel powerless to deal with difficult situations. We will get into some techniques in the following chapters on how to handle our reactive state so that we can develop a proactive position instead of just letting everything get to us.

Focus on Progress, Not Perfection

Perfectionism is a good thing sometimes. It can push us toward greatness instead of settling for mediocrity. It can also be an obstacle that gets in the way of making steady progress in our lives. Afraid of making mistakes, we try to do everything perfectly the first time to avoid failing. In the end we end up stalling and put off taking any kind of action.

We have a strong tendency to do things perfectly or not at all. When reading through this material, put aside the perfectionist and focus on progress that moves you ahead one step at a time. Five things done well are better than one thing done perfectly (and it is never perfect anyway).

Perfectionism is a lie that keeps you stuck. So step back and take it easy. Give yourself space to grow. Allow yourself to make mistakes. I am not perfect; you are not perfect. But you can be perfectly okay.

Keep an Open Mind

In this book, I ask that you have an open mind to the ideas and thoughts I am going to share with you. You do not have to accept everything, and not everything may apply to you. But when you are working through this and something suddenly clicks or stops you in your tracks, it could be a sign that something needs more attention.

Focus on the areas of your life that need adjustments. Work to replace what you have to so that you can move forward with your life. Keep in mind that you can create the lifestyle you want. You are not inadequate or flawed, as you may have been led to believe. Keep reminding yourself that you are an exceptional human being and you deserve the best.

Get into the habit of talking to yourself every morning before you leave the house. Practice having this silent conversation with yourself several times a day for relaxation. Focus on calming the voices inside your head that ramble on without meaning. By keeping an open mind, you will feel more relaxed and focused, and this will help you to deal with everyday situations that you find difficult.

Give Yourself Time to Heal

I do not want you to get overwhelmed with the process. Personal growth is a work in progress. Your success takes a series of small steps over a period of time. It is not the size of the jump you make that counts, but the number of steps you take along the way. There is no rush. Steady persistence is the key.

This is important, because if you are anything like I was, you will end up quitting soon, as I did many times in the past. I started something, expecting to have amazing results in a week. But when I was not completely transformed I gave up. I started to look for the next quick solution. This led back to my old self-defeating behaviors that worked in the short term because they were reliable.

Just remember, there are no quick fixes. By taking action just a little bit every day, you will build up a powerful reservoir of confidence, self-esteem, and discipline. Take things slowly and give yourself room to explore.

Visualize Your New Outcome

Start to think about what you want to do with your life. Imagine yourself overcoming rejection and feelings of inferiority. See yourself doing, being, and having what you once only dreamt about. You can start to do this right now. Get focused and look at where you are today.

If you are in a bad place emotionally, then that is where you are. It is okay. Everyone has to start from somewhere. We do not have to wait for a perfect moment or the right circumstances to begin; just start from where you are at. The journey ahead of you is unfolding, as it needs to.

Lao Tzu said, "A journey of 1,000 miles begins with a single step." I want you to think of every day from now on as the next step and focus on the goal you are moving toward.

Do not look back and wish that things had been different. They will never be different. You can start to look at the situation differently. Think of every day as a new beginning full of opportunities. What happened yesterday or ten years ago is in the past. This does not mean you should just pretend nothing happened, but know that you are not the only one with a past that was not perfect. What you do today is what matters.

Visualize the life that you have always wanted to have, and not the one you feel stuck with. Visualize yourself doing, being, and living the best possible way you can. Start to think deeply about the direction in which you are now heading. Imagine where you could be in two years, five years, and ten years down the road by committing to a plan of action. The reality you can imagine is the life you can have, if you really want it.

You can choose your own way right now. You can stand up and say no more. You can set your own standards for living instead of the self-imposed limitations that were thrown onto you.

Do not put your life on hold anymore; it is time to make a serious shift in the way you think, feel, and take massive action.

BREAKING THROUGH OBSTACLES: A 4-STEP FORMULA

"History has demonstrated that the most notable winners usually encountered heartbreaking obstacles before they triumphed. They won because they refused to become discouraged by their defeats."

—B. C. Forbes

Obstacles are barriers that stand between you and the fulfillment of your dreams. To get from where you are today to the place you desire to be in the not-too- distant future, you will have to face life's challenging roadblocks along the way.

Most of these obstacles can be overcome with a few simple strategies. More difficult challenges require an advanced approach. This could be a shift in personal values, the adoption of new beliefs, or developing a deeper level of wisdom and mindfulness.

In some cases, therapy is required to overcome issues that may be blocking you from reaching your goals.

If you are serious about achieving your dreams and are willing to go to any lengths, you will endure difficulties in which courage and confidence is challenged, beliefs are questioned, and unresolved trauma is confronted. In this place of fear and uncertainty, you will have to face the most terrifying obstacle of all: yourself.

You must prepare yourself to dig in and push through the problems blocking your direct path to freedom. Only by facing obstacles will you be able to make progress. Unfortunately, many people falter as soon as they hit the first wall and realize there's no instant solution that can solve their problems.

An obstacle is blocking your path and appears insurmountable. Unless you can find a way to get past this hurdle, you will always be stuck by challenges that appear larger than you. When you find yourself at this crossroad, remember there is no problem or difficulty too complex that cannot be resolved.

Your success in any situation is measured by your performance in working through problems. If there is a way to avoid dealing with the problem, your first instinct may be to disregard it, bury it, or try to pass it on to someone else.

Either way, you will only seek to defeat yourself. That which you do not confront is unresolved. Even if it is resolved by someone else, this won't help you grow. You must take care of your own weeds in the garden. They are still your weeds—even if someone else pulls them out.

When you pass the buck to someone else, instead of making a real effort to solve the situation, you end up disempowering yourself. You are doing the other person a favor by giving them the opportunity to solve what you passed on. There's nothing wrong with asking for help but be intentional in conquering your own issues.

Life's obstacles present an opportunity to strengthen

yourself and become more confident as you defeat your own limitations. One of the greatest measures of successful people is their ability to transcend life's difficulties and overcome the roadblocks that threaten to hold them back. Successful people stand up to challenges that threaten their goals and dreams.

External and Internal Obstacles

> *"Unless you try to do something beyond what you have already mastered, you will never grow."*
>
> —Ronald E. Osborn

I have divided obstacles into two categories: **external** and **internal**. We largely create circumstances in our lives through our emotion, thought, action, interaction with people, and the quality of our relationships.

The problems we create because of our direct influence are called internal obstacles. The other set of obstacles is external, and in most cases, has nothing to do with us directly. However, we may be connected to such obstacles, not by choice but by duty or responsibility to seek solutions.

External Obstacles

External obstacles are the unpredictable events thrown in your path when you least expect them. They are created by the situations, circumstances, and natural events that are beyond your control.

Whether it is a global crisis that starts on the opposite side of the world or an ill family member who needs your immediate attention, external obstacles challenge your ability to deal with a situation that is not entirely of your own making.

There is very little you can do to prevent these things from happening. However, you can do everything in your control to make the circumstances more favorable. This could mean reaching out to someone who really needs your help. Or, being pulled into a situation either at work or at home where a problem exists, and you are expected to provide a successful outcome for other parties.

You may not have created a particular problem, but you could still be a part of the solution.

When a situation that you didn't create arises, instead of responding with fear or by deciding it's "not my problem," condition yourself to adopt a different approach. Consider this a valuable opportunity to step up and take charge. If you feel afraid of the problem, let yourself feel that fear. Take direct action in the face of what frightens you. Your fearful emotions do not have to control your actions. You can control your emotions by *doing* something.

You can respond to any situation. If you choose to disregard a certain problem, it will continue to exist. The best time to determine how to deal with an obstacle is when it stands between you and all your hopes and dreams. You may face a situation in which you're asked to find a solution to a problem, and others could be looking to you for guidance.

Regardless of whether the problem is a situation in your company, at home, or in a personal relationship, always ask yourself the following:

What can I do in this situation?
How can I make a difference here?
What actions could I take right now that everyone else is avoiding?

These questions create a higher level of personal empowerment as you start to think about possible solutions.

When you seek solutions to obstacles keeping you stuck, you empower yourself. When you rely on someone else to figure out the answers, you empower them. If you work together to overcome a barrier, you empower each other.

You can develop new methods and solutions for tackling these barriers when they appear and pose as obstacles in your path.

External obstacles include things such as the decisions of others and how they impact you, global economic crisis, war, natural disasters and illness.

You can decide how to handle the situation. Will you let it influence you in a negative manner, draining your energy day after day as the circumstances of the world shape your future? Instead, will you take action to seek out a solution to make the best of the situation at hand?

You always have a choice, in any situation, to do something. Take the lead when you have to and step back to let others deal with the crisis when that's the best thing to do. As long as you are aware of the difference, you can decide either way.

Internal Obstacles

Internal obstacles are problems or conditions that are created through your direct involvement. It may be a situation arising from an unresolved issue, a difficult relationship, or a crisis related to work.

These obstacles can be very threatening because of the personal emotional ties we have to them. With external obstacles, it is much easier when you can acknowledge that you had nothing to do with creating this situation. But personal obstacles are more emotional and tied closely to your feelings of rejection and failure.

We all face countless internal obstacles. Many of these obstacles are small and harmless, so they go unnoticed. Other obstacles, however, may take over our lives. If they are not controlled or removed, their manifestation could make you miserable. These self-defeating behaviors grow from within and threaten to destroy you. They harm you spiritually and negatively influence your confidence and your ability to take a proactive stance.

If they aren't confronted, they act like slow poison. When this happens, we become powerless, foolish, and fatigued. In our efforts to avoid pain and suffering caused by obstacles created by our self-defeating behaviors, we may turn to other methods of escapism (drugs, alcohol, excessive shopping) to relieve our suffering inflicted by this internal enemy. Internal obstacles include things like addictions, grief, trauma, negative thinking and more.

Obstacles that are hidden from view are the most difficult to overcome. Our greatest enemy is within us and remains elusive until strong intervention measures are taken.

Once you have confronted your greatest fears, you will have taken the first step to victory. The stranglehold that these problems have on your life will be defeated and the pathway to a new way of living will appear before you. This is your pathway to freedom. When you face your greatest trial with courage and faith, you are free to walk this path.

Facing your fears and personal demons gives you great strength. When you refuse to be defeated, the chains that bind you are released.

Whether you have an addiction, or you habitually think negatively, the power to change these behaviors lies within you. In the end, you are only as weak as you believe yourself to be.

Obstacles Have a Five-Fold Purpose

> *"Happiness is dependent on self-discipline. We are the biggest obstacles to our own happiness. It is much easier to do battle with society and with others than to fight our own nature."*
>
> —Dennis Prager

An obstacle is not a roadblock; it is a necessary element that serves a purpose. Obstacles help us grow. We tend to think problems will prevent us from moving ahead. Instead, it is by developing solutions to overcome challenges that the greatest growth is achieved.

Here are five reasons why obstacles matter and why we should embrace them as tools that can help us evolve.

1. Obstacles contribute to growth and development

Develop the attitude that every challenging situation carries an opportunity for you to become stronger. Create a deeper awareness of why this particular problem has come into your life.

It is important to acknowledge that obstacles exist to enable us to evolve and make progress. This builds character, boosts courage, and gives you a deeper feeling of satisfaction once you have effectively worked through a difficult period.

2. Obstacles serve to increase self-confidence and boost self-esteem

We feel a sense of deep fulfillment by overcoming challenges. This increases confidence and strengthens the belief that nothing is impossible. Instead of being powerless, you become empowered. You develop a strong character.

With every victory, your confidence moves up a notch, making you less fearful of the future. Remember that most people fail because they don't believe in themselves, not because they lack ability.

3. Meeting new challenges expands opportunities

You can become the master of problem-solving only by facing adversity and the things in life that oppose your ideals or chosen path. Your greatest challenge is to deal with difficult people or unpleasant situations.

These challenges give you an opportunity to become something today that you weren't yesterday, to face problems and find solutions. Your greatest victory lies in facing your deepest fears.

4. Overcoming obstacles puts us in line with our life's purpose

Dealing with obstacles aligns us with things that are important in our lives. What appears to be a roadblock is actually a tool for enhancing focus and bringing us back to the path that leads to fulfillment. Meet challenges head on, find solutions, and when you can't find the answers you're looking for right away, take the time to explore other possible solutions.

Weigh your decisions carefully. Brainstorm options. Meditate and focus on whatever has led you to this place. Perceive every challenge as a stepping stone to a new level of awareness that draws you closer to your purpose, enabling you to stay on track.

Once you have managed to effectively remove a roadblock, it becomes a part of your life. You don't just throw it away and forget about it. Instead, forge a relationship with each victory. The obstacles in your life have a purpose and, once you have faced them and effectively handled the situation, your life's purpose become clearer.

5. Obstacles serve as your greatest teachers.

Obstacles are not necessarily hindrances designed to cause failure. However, your perception of a significant problem or misfortune in many cases is disillusioned. The obstacle that stands in your way serves as your greatest teacher. You learn the deepest lessons in life by facing the situations that challenge you and by overcoming these opposing forces. Remember that the tougher the challenge, the greater the reward and more valuable the lesson.

Facing the Thirty-Foot Wall

When faced with a situation that we don't know how to deal with, the initial instinct is to react with negative resistance. We approach the solution from an angle of powerlessness. You may say things like, "Well, it's not my problem! I had nothing to do with this!" or catch yourself complaining about the situation and coming up with reasons why it happened, how it could have been avoided, and who is to blame.

Complaining is always a complete waste of resources. It only adds to the problem and offers nothing in exchange.

Complaining about something or someone only makes the situation more unbearable for both the complainer and the people listening to them. You may think that you are getting something off your chest or releasing your frustration surrounding a particular incident, but if you carefully observe how you feel afterward, you'll probably realize that you feel even more stressed and angry. Nothing will have been resolved. Only negative emotions would have been unleashed.

Many of the ways that we deal with problems are based on our experiences, traumas, and old ways that support our limiting beliefs. When we don't know what to do, we react based on old methods that no longer work. We tend to fall into our old patterns, especially when it comes to problem solving, as a means of dealing with our own fears and insecurities. We resist the problem until it becomes someone else's problem or is buried under all the lies we tell ourselves.

One of the first things we tend to do is label the problem with a negative attitude. If it is a person, we come up with damaging labels for them. Labeling something attaches the blame to a person or situation. However, labeling not only disempowers the person being labeled, it also disempowers you.

If a difficult situation arises, avoid the labeling game. For many people, their first reaction is to strap a label on the problem and walk away. They distance themselves from the obstacle as if to say, "There, I just took care of it. Next?"

When faced with a challenge, focus on controlling your initial reactions to the problem. Instead of picking up the phone and launching a complaint session, think of effective solutions you could try to make the situation better. Instead of reacting negatively and saying there is no solution, first identify exactly what the difficulty is, and then mind map the solutions to reach a conclusion.

Try to find solutions to everything. Take time to think things through. Brainstorm ideas and talk with people positively instead of labeling or gossiping. This is "obstacle avoidance," and it is the most unproductive approach you can take.

Perceive every problem as an opportunity to expand your growth. Listen to what your emotions are telling you and not your mind. The mind is full of ego and rarely works to resolve anything when left to its own devices. When you follow your heart in any situation, everything will be the better for it.

The Formula: A Four-Step Process

> *"Concern yourself more with accepting responsibility than with assigning blame. Let the possibilities inspire you more than the obstacles discourage you."*
>
> —Ralph Marston

There is an effective formula or process that can be applied to almost any challenging situation or difficulty you are facing. When confronted with a problem that seems too big to conquer, you can find a way to overcome it by using the four-step process below.

1. Identify the obstacle

Describe the obstacle in one sentence. Do you want to buy a house, but you don't have enough money? Do you have to speak with your boss about a problem with your work? Is your son or daughter experiencing a problem at school and they need your help? Are you working on a project that is over budget and behind schedule?

No matter what the situation is, the first step to working toward a solution is to identify it. Write it out on paper to make it real. Don't keep anything in your head and try to work it out. That's the worst place for a challenge to exist. Then, once you have identified the problem with absolute clarity....

2. Mind map potential solutions

Now that you have clearly defined the obstacle, it is easier to draw ideas on what actions to take. For the second step, create a "branch of ideas," or a mind map of possible solutions. By putting your ideas to paper, you can see with greater clarity the solution to overcoming your obstacles.

People get stuck when they hold those ideas in their head. The mind has a way of latching onto a problem and making it bigger by focusing on the problem instead of the way out.

You can now write in point form as many possible solutions as you can think of.

3. Select the best choice

Next, from the list of options, choose the best one. Write down the best solution and work toward taking immediate action. It may be that the obstacle requires several solutions.

In this case, you can prioritize the options in the order of importance. Take direct action on the first choice and once complete, move to the next possible solution on your list. Keep working through it until you have successfully overcome the problem.

4. Follow up on the outcome.

After applying the formula to your situation, you may not have an immediate outcome. The application of your solutions may take time to work. The final stage is to follow up on the results.

Did you get the outcome you wanted? Did you experience a different result than what you expected? If you didn't get what you were hoping for, continue to apply other solutions. Just because something didn't deliver the first time doesn't mean the situation is hopeless. For every obstacle you face, there is a way to overcome it.

Action Plan

1. What obstacles are holding you back right now? Do you have a plan for getting past them? Apply the above formula to help you develop solutions.

2. Everyone has at least one self-defeating behavior that challenges them. Write down your self- defeating behavior and the steps you plan to take to overcome this behavior.
3. Create a mind map of solutions for this scenario and put your ideas into action.
4. Next, write down an internal obstacle you're currently facing. Subsequently, think about this obstacle and brainstorm solutions.
5. Write about an external obstacle you had to face. Were you successful in dealing with it? If so, how did you do it? If not, what would you have done differently?

WHAT IT TAKES TO WIN
(AND MASTER YOUR GREATEST GIFT)

You were not born with gifts. You develop your gifts in this life and build the talent needed to turn your talent into dreams.

Talent is not about being the best, the smartest in the room, or the luckiest in the right place at the right time. The definition of better talent—or a genius—is that person who goes the extra mile, does one more rep at the gym, runs another mile when the rest crossed the finished mile.

Michael Jordan was one of the best basketball players in the NBA. Many say he was gifted and talented. But that's not why he's the best. He was also first on the court and last to leave. There is risk in becoming great at what you do, but it's not what you think. The risk is in saying NO to the expectations we are pressured to live by.

If you have a 9-5 job, does that mean you can only work 9-5? If you make $40,000 a year, does that mean you can only earn this amount? If you are told "You'll never amount to anything," does that mean you have to believe it?

By committing to pushing yourself beyond what the world is expecting, you develop a natural talent for being better because you're doing more, getting better, and stacking the odds in your favor.

Nobody is "born" lucky. Yes, many are born with more and

many more are born with much less. But the circumstances do not define your future, or limit you to what you can achieve.

You can always create the circumstances and opportunity you want. When someone gets a "lucky break" in life, I want to know what actions this person took to make that opportunity show up in the first place.

Never give up when the road gets difficult. It is in the moment of pain that you begin to grow.

Muhammad Ali once said, "I start counting the sit ups when they begin to hurt."

Instead of pushing yourself to your limits, push beyond the limits of your mind. When you're living life according to a set of parameters that says "I always put in (XX) number of hours or reps, nothing is stopping you from doing one more, pushing another rep or making ten more calls than anybody else on the floor.

You have the power to define your own limitations, and if you believe in your limits, they are yours. Strive for limitless and you do the unimaginable.

If someone tells you "that's impossible," they are always right. But it's impossible for them, not for you.

Most people give up on their dreams too soon. They try hard for a few years and if they don't succeed will bounce back to doing predictable actions.

Predictable outcomes are comfortable. We don't fail like failures because we let go of those high expectations. There is less pressure. No stress. But the stress and pressure come later, when you realize that you're approaching the end of your life with very little fulfillment.

People will tell you to "take it easy" or "stop pushing yourself too hard." It's not that they don't care, they would rather not see you struggle. But friends, the success is in the struggle. You can struggle now or struggle later.

When you do what is expected, some people are less threatened or intimidated. You are treated differently when you do more and be better than the rest by pushing past the barriers holding you back. If there is a wall in front of you that says, "Break limitations here", in your mind I want you to take a sledgehammer and knock down that wall.

Your thoughts and beliefs are that mental sledgehammer. These are the weapons of your mind. Too many people forget they have the tools now to break all these mental blocks. But they are scared to pick up that hammer and get to work.

You don't need permission. You are already born great; now you need to maximize your greatness and push to see how far you can really go. Become hungry and obsessed with needing to know what is on the other side of that fear.

You know what it is on this side of it; what is waiting for you on that other side of the river enshrouded in fog that you can't see. The only way to find out is to cross those raging rapids and get to the other side.

Are you willing to do whatever it takes to get there? Are you hungry enough to know just how far you can go in the next twenty years?

> *"I always had a philosophy which I got from my father. He used to say, 'Listen. God gave to you the gift to play football. This is your gift from God. If you take care of your health, if you are in good shape all the time, with your gift from God no one will stop you, but you must be prepared."*
>
> —Pele

Crush the limiting mindset and replace it with a limitless mindset. Break your limiting beliefs and replace it with beliefs of limitless goals and dreams.

How do you do this?

Imagine the life you are going to have by doing whatever it takes to get there. If you do one more rep a day, save five more dollars instead of spending it, and show up earlier than everyone else and stay five minutes later, that is the difference that builds **massive momentum**.

Your untrained mind will default to surrendering to good enough when the process begins to hurt. That is when you do one more. You push a little past your pain. Make it hurt for one more second, one more mile, one more phone call.

To get the things you have always wanted, you must be willing to do what the rest of the people aren't willing to do. This attitude and mindset shift is the difference that makes champions.

The champion mindset is a winning mindset. You are the champion in the arena of your own life. The difference between going from here to there is the force of effort you exert to move there.

Are you doing just enough to get by, or are you ready to do everything and anything it takes?

Being "gifted" or diversely "talented" is the outcome of intentional action fueled by a purpose-driven mindset. It isn't working harder for the sake of working, or putting in more time because your manager says, "We are putting in an extra 30 minutes today".

It is your intentional decision to take maximum action. It is doing your best without prompting or the promise of a reward for "sticking around." This—I promise you—is the key that makes the difference.

It's not about becoming better than everyone else or, beating the competition, or doing it for money or fame. It's about becoming better than who you were the day before. It's about defeating the person you have always been, so you can become the greatest version of yourself that you once deemed impossible.

Being more and doing more is better. But not buying more things and wasting more time on worthless activities that go nowhere. You know what these are.

The goal is generating massive growth by being growth focused and creating a growth mindset. You grow exponentially by pushing past the limits set by a world obsessed with boundaries and systems designed to keep you trapped.

You cannot always change external circumstances, but you have direct influence over your own choices.

When someone tells you to stop pushing so hard because you might wear out, you decide to give in or go the extra distance. If you work for an employer who pays you $40,000 a year and they tell you "that's what your time (and 261 days a year) is worth", you create a side business to double your income in that year.

When you hear your friends invite you out again Saturday night to drink and celebrate the weekend, you decide to join them, or stay home alone and work on your passion.

Do one more. Do ten more. Maximum Momentum is built into your mindset and becomes the fuel driving you closer towards your goals.

When you do this, you don't need confidence building strategies. This is the path to relentless confidence. Accumulate your time invested and, over the months and years to come, you have just 100x your momentum. Continue on this path and in five years your momentum is like that tsunami that started as a small wave until it is 100 meters high and becomes unstoppable.

I'll share with you my definition of pain: It will be getting to the end of my life in 20, 30 or 50 years and realizing that I didn't do everything I could have done to win. I did what was expected and everything I accumulated is the result of fulfilling those expectations.

Your fulfillment in life will always be measured by the amount of energy and intensity invested in doing what you love to do. This doesn't mean you will always enjoy it, but the hard days now are of putting in the work and getting small wins puts you in the front of the race.

Did you know that 25—30% of runners who join a marathon will give up after it's announced the #1 runner has crossed the line? The real champions don't always win the race or come in first. But they finish the race. Giving up because you don't win the big prize means that you'll give up on everything else. It becomes your default mindset. You don't always have to be the fastest or best or most intelligent. You only need to be committed to chiseling your mindset into an indestructible mechanism designed for mastery.

The definition of mastery is an individual totally committed to the path of constant and never-ending improvement. I used to believe a master was a perfect being with all the answers to the universe. But this isn't true. You are a master on a dedicated path to mastery the moment you choose this way of life.

This way of life becomes your greatest calling.

Nobody can take that away from you. When Viktor Frankl was forced to survive in a concentration camp from 1943-1945, after losing his family in the camps, he continued to march on. He forged an unbreakable mindset for not only survival but winning over his captors.

He had said years later: *"Everything can be taken from a person but one thing: the last of the human freedoms—to choose one's attitude in any given set of circumstances, to choose one's own way."*

When your friends ask you "what is your secret to getting ahead," you can say, "I put in the extra time and always do whatever it takes to break against any and all barriers."

People will call you obsessive and unnatural. That is good, that is what you want. Success is not a linear process. You must be so obsessed to get there that your mind becomes like the power of the ocean, crashing into the rocks again and again until it shapes the formations of that rock. The change is never noticeable until thousands of years later those rocks have been transformed.

Stack your small wins. It is the small wins that matter over an extended period of time. Too often we ignore the small wins and focus on the big prize. But all your small wins accumulated bring that big prize closer.

Count your small wins as essential victories. If you're training for a marathon and you run for 3 km a day, that's a small win. Completing the marathon is your big win, but you only get there through daily practice and adding up all those days you put in 3 km to condition your body for winning.

How long do you continue this habit of doing more? I would install this habit of doing more, and make it a part of my being, doing and ultimate mindset. Your greatest gift isn't always your natural talent.

It is the one thing that fulfills you and fills you up with so much passion, your drive to be the best is unbreakable. When people call you "obsessed" you can say, "that's right, I am. What are you obsessed about?"

I encourage you now to choose your way, to make this your story, and no matter what you hear, or other people's beliefs are placed in front of you, only you control the internal mechanisms of your own life. You have the key to unlocking your greatest gifts. Where is this key? Are you still waiting for someone to hand it over to you?

Use that key to unlock your door to a new universe. Do it now, and don't let shame get in the way.

Take the **RED** pill and begin your journey down the rabbit hole. See where it goes. Cross the river and discover everything you've ever dreamed of on the other side.

To win big, get small wins, become obsessed about your greatest passion, and always do the thing most are not willing to do.

HOW TO CREATE PURPOSE FOR YOUR LIFE

Six Strategies for Building Purpose in Your Life

"The first principle of ethical power is Purpose. By purpose, I don't mean your objective or intention—something toward which you are always striving. Purpose is something bigger. It is the picture you have of yourself—the kind of person you want to be or the kind of life you want to lead."

—Ken Blanchard

1. Forge an Iron-Clad Character

Fortitude of character defines destiny and sets your fate on many levels. Strength of character opens up the endless roads of opportunity and experiences you encounter on the journey. Everything that happens to you stems from the force of character you impress upon the world.

Character becomes the foundation for a life well lived; it defines you through the actions you take or fail to take, the values you choose to live by, and the attitude you project towards people and situations. Fate is determined, not by chance or a predetermined path but fortitude of character. It is a decision to dedicate yourself to the principle of constant and never ending improvement.

Each of us is born into this world with uniqueness of character. Nobody is like you. As spiritual beings born of a mission to discover the purpose of living, you are given the responsibility to care for the soul's character. There are no limits when it comes to creating yourself.

The limits we face are self-imposed and the levels of success or failure are determined by how well you are able to tend to the "garden of the soul" that is your character. It requires special care and obedience, love and appreciation to expand and grow. This "garden of the soul", so to speak, requires regular maintenance and discipline so that it can function properly. If you neglect to pull out the "weeds" that fester in your mind, defects of character become the dominant force in your life.

A character that is neglected breaks down over time, but if you have a vision of the person you desire to become, your subconscious will work to create the real you in the exact way that you desire. Be clear in the values you hold most sacred; replace your weak habits with positive actions that build and create your life.

Always be working on something new and exciting. Get excited about the person you have the potential of becoming instead of just settling for who you ended up as.

If you are already totally happy with the way you are, reach out to others and help them. There is always room for improvement no matter who you are. Even some of the greatest characters that ever walked this earth never stopped seeking the path to self- improvement.

2. Decide, Commit, And Take Action!

Strong decision making, when combined with a commitment to a specific objective, is a valuable skill for acquiring success. Likewise, failing to make a decision and committing to a course of action puts you in a position of weakness.

The reason for this is simple: *If you fail to make clear- cut decisions, you place decision-making power in the hands of others.*

The inability to make swift, confident decisions is like handing over the keys to your new sports car and saying to someone: "Here, this car is too much for me, you drive!" The ability to make decisions that commit you to an objective puts you in the driver's seat of your life. Believe in yourself to make the right decisions and, once you do, quit worrying about the outcomes and trust that they will take care of themselves.

People struggle with indecision because they can't commit to the outcome that the decision will manifest. They don't want to accept responsibility should things not go as expected. There is too much at stake. They might lose money, position, pride, or suffer embarrassment if they fail. Terrified of choosing poorly, they don't choose anything. Have you ever made an important decision and afterwards second-guessed yourself for days or weeks?

Someone once suggested to me to make decisions quickly, within ten seconds or less, whenever possible. By doing this, you eliminate procrastination and sleep better knowing that you have made a decision and the outcome now rests in the hands of the universe. If you sleep on a decision that needs to be made, you probably won't sleep much at all.

Train yourself to decide quickly. Indecisiveness builds fear and anxiety that creates passiveness and, ultimately, failure to reach your goals. Remember: *If you can't decide, someone else will decide for you.* Take a stand and accept from the outset that not everything is going to manifest exactly as you hope it should and have faith in the knowledge that things will work out exactly as they are supposed to.

You should plan for success, but plan for the unexpected as well. Accept this as part of the decision-making process. Here are three simple steps for making decisions more effectively:

a. **Make your decision as quickly as possible.** If you require more information to gather knowledge, research the problem or ask for advice. Once all the facts have been gathered and there's nothing more to do, decide quickly. Do not try to guess or control the outcome.

b. **Commit to your decision.** Unless there is some danger involved in your decision or the circumstances have changed, second-guessing and attempting to alter your decision only diminishes your faith in yourself and the universe. Right or wrong, for better or for worse, acknowledge that you have taken action on the basis of a decision and that it is the best that you can do for now.

c. **Take immediate action!** As soon as you decide something, such as changing your job or quitting a habit that no longer supports your greater purpose, you must take immediate action. Momentum moves you in the direction you want to go—forward! A decision without follow-up action is meaningless.

If you want to get the results that you desire, the weight of your decision must be met with the same weight in action. Of course, there are some big decisions that do require time to make because you may need to consult people for advice or research the problem. If the situation permits, it's perfectly fine to take time out to think it over. Then, as soon as you are sure of what it is that you want, decide quickly and move on.

3. Develop a Positive Winning Attitude!

You have complete control over the cultivation of a positive winning attitude. Regardless of what happens in this world, whether it is a war or a global economic depression, nothing should break or change your attitude towards life. Only you have the power to do that. To possess a winning mind is a choice, and it is the best choice that you can make. Tell yourself that, irrespective of what the situation may be, maintaining a healthy outlook by cultivating a healthy mind and creating a positive attitude is the only way to gain mastery over the mind.

If you maintain a healthy outlook, the natural laws of the universe will enable you to attract the right opportunities for ensuring your success. If you maintain a steady, winning attitude, everything that you desire will align itself to be yours. Likewise, a negative and pessimistic attitude that is full of anger, envy, greed, dishonesty and fear will yield negative consequences and, ultimately, failure.

It is an unconditional truth that a negative attitude produces failure, and eventually negative results lead to the spiraling of an undesirable way of life. Remember: *You are not a victim of circumstances. You are the creator of your own circumstances.*

It is your great purpose that feeds this mental energy and stimulates your positive thinking, thereby reinforcing your winning attitude.

4. Create a Healthy Balance by Identifying What Matters Most

It is essential to maintain a healthy balance in the critical areas of your life. It takes practice and discipline to develop this "life balance." You must know exactly what it is that is most important, what your priority values are and what you value the most; subsequently, make a plan to spend an adequate amount of time building a quality relationship with the most meaningful elements of your life.

Take some time to enjoy the things that you might have been neglecting. Spend some of your hard-earned money on something that you have always wanted. Enjoy the early years of your children before they are gone forever. Have a dinner party and invite your closest friends. And most of all, take adequate time off to rest. I know people who work from morning to night, crawl home exhausted, only to wake up the next day and do it all over again.

This pattern, repeated over many years, is exhausting and shaves years off your life. Regardless of how much money you are making or how far up the ladder you are climbing, it will not replace the lost time you could have spent with family and friends, building real relationships with the only people who truly matter. Besides, you might get to the top of the ladder someday only to realize you are the only one there! Creating more free time enables you to make more time for your family and focus on your goals and building your life while pursuing other interests that could lead to greater opportunities.

5. Develop Innovative Ideas

Ideas are the tracks to success. Innovative ideas give rise to the sparks of creativity that stimulate the imagination, impressing visions and thoughts onto the subconscious mind. This occurs even as we sleep. In other words, ideas *turn on* your mind, opening the doors to a level of creative thinking that didn't exist before.

In the first moment that an idea is conceived, it is either accepted or rejected by your purpose-driven mind. If the idea strongly contributes to your personal mission, it must be put into action immediately. The idea must grow from the moment it is conceived. If the idea positively contributes to your great purpose, it becomes a building block towards the advancement of growth and development.

As your mind develops and expands from one state to another, ideas occur more vividly. Although you may once have had ideas that appeared out of confusion or uncertainty, every thought and idea that you conceive after you have developed a purpose-driven mind state contributes to building purpose into your every action. Your actions then begin serving your life's purpose and mission.

By creating this new mindset through concentration of mind energy, your ideas become like a wildfire that burns slowly at first, but soon rages out of control. Make a habit of writing down your ideas as soon as they occur because, hours or days later, when you try to recall that particular idea that you had, you will find that you can't. It has moved beyond your realm of thought and can no longer be retrieved.

6. Become an authority in one specific area of your life and work

One of the most powerful ways to express great purpose is through your work. You might be asking yourself, "What is my life's work? What was I put on this earth to do?" Perhaps you are a painter, mechanic, musician, writer, psychologist, dancer, poet, pilot, veterinarian, business executive, athlete, entrepreneur, or world-class performer.

Regardless of your profession, working hard at something that you love to do is one of the most substantial ways to express your great purpose. It is how you show the world who you truly are.

In your quest for labor that is worthy of your time, it is important to find an occupation that you are passionate about. Don't just settle for what you can get—pursue the things that you crave to master. Turn your occupation into your greatest obsession; and if what you are doing isn't what you want to do, make the necessary changes that will make you the happiest.

Always do what you want to do and not what others expect of you. As your purpose unfolds, you will notice a definite increase in the possibilities surrounding you. Once you discover a field of work that you are passionate about, it suddenly won't seem like work anymore. Doing what you love to do *and getting paid for it* is the very essence of building a successful life full of fulfillment and genuine happiness.

DEVELOP YOUR OBSESSION
(AND DO WHATEVER IT TAKES)

"If something is important enough, even if the odds are against you, you should still do it."

—Elon Musk

Years ago, I awakened my obsession when I read Tony Robbins's amazing book *Awaken the Giant Within*. I discovered the book by accident; something told me to pick it up, and with the last twenty bucks I had, I walked out of that bookstore with a book that would change the course of my life.

Within weeks I was writing down my goals, practicing positive affirmations, and talking about success and the things that I was going to do. I turned my addiction for chaos into an addiction for learning. The more I discovered and implemented, the hungrier I became for knowledge and growth.

I would write out my goals over and over, refining my mission and purpose. The more I did this, the more I recognized patterns. My obsession was awakening and telling me what to do next. I felt like I had been a lost ship on the ocean in the middle of a storm and suddenly, there was light on land guiding me carefully toward safe shores.

Within weeks, I uncovered my deep-seated dream of wanting to travel the world, learn a new language, and write books that would help people achieve success. I was obsessed with my dream. I started planning my escape. I decided that one year from that day, I was getting on an airplane and leaving my safety net of work, relationships, friends, and family to pursue an obsession with living a great life.

At first, a lot of "what if" questions came to my mind. What if I ran out of money after I started traveling? What if I failed and had to start all over again? What if …? I realized that these questions were the wrong questions to ask because they only built fear. I started to ask "how" and "what" questions instead. "How would I get to Thailand? What would I first do when I got there?"

I pinned up my vision board on my wall. I put up my goals, positivity quotes, and anything else I could find. I knew I had to start living the dream in my mind first before it became my reality.

To build your "No Punches Pulled" approach to life, you need to develop an obsession for your dreams—you need to awaken and commit to it. Make yourself obsessed with your success. Make yourself obsessed with becoming your best.

You can only be obsessed with something if you truly love it, whether it's a job, a target net worth number, a painting, a degree, a fitness goal, or a relationship. Only if you truly care about something will you persist against the odds. Remember—it should be *you* that's obsessed with your goal, and not someone else influencing you.

With such obsession, *success is certain.*

Learning from the heroes

Think of the most successful people in the world. I promise you none of them got where there wanted to be without being obsessed with their dreams, visions and goals. It's said that Muhammed Ali used to repeat "I'm the best, I'm the best" because he wanted to believe it himself first, so that he could go out and beat the best. If you truly want to be all in and will stop at nothing, you need to light that fire within you that will help you crush everything that gets in your way.

"You must become your own champion and cheerleader before anyone else starts cheering you on."

Michael Jordan is the best basketball player on the planet because he became obsessed with becoming the best and let nothing get in his way. Elon Musk is making history by building the future because he became obsessed with creating the future, and no matter how many failures he endured, he continued to push the boundaries of space and science.

Best-selling author and world-class speaker **Mel Robbins**, in her book *The High Five Habit*, says that "the #1 reason people fail to reach their goals is that they don't believe they are worthy of having them. They are not obsessed enough to make it happen."

Make a list of the famous people you know; there are hundreds and thousands of them. From classical composers Mozart and Bach to modern sports figures such as Babe Ruth and Muhammad Ali, actors and movie directors, Steve Jobs and Serena Williams, Bill Gates, Jim Henson, Steven Spielberg, John Williams, Stephen King, J. K. Rowling, Wayne Gretzky, and Mark Zuckerberg. Obsession had all of them. They wouldn't be where they are today, if it were not for that obsession to go beyond where everyone else stopped pushing the boundary. That is what obsession does to you.

Using your obsession to become a master

Your obsession aligns with and fuels your purpose—the reason you were born. Stephen King is one of the greatest writers of our time. He has written over 70 books and sold over 450 million copies. But he wouldn't have succeeded at just about anything; it was his purpose in life to be a great writer. Serena Williams is one of the greatest tennis players who ever lived, but it is tennis she mastered. Not golf or bowling nor tennis.

Take any super-achiever and look at what they have mastered. You will see a singular driving purpose and an all-consuming obsession behind their success. You will see raw grit: a potent combination of **passion**, **determination**, and **perseverance**.

No such thing as an overnight success

In a culture wrapped tightly around social media, people get carried away by "overnight sensations." They look at winners in amazement and chalk up their success to a born talent or an unfair competitive advantage. They'll say some just got lucky.

While it's certainly true that these people got lucky breaks, it's also true that they set up everything to make luck happen. They were fully prepared when their opportunities presented themselves; they had trained for it for years, if not for decades.

The difference between obsession and motivation

Obsession and motivation are similar, but not the same. Motivation rides entirely on emotion; it's there one minute and gone the next. It's unreliable. Obsession, on the other hand, is closer to hyper-focus. You live, breathe, and act according to the very thing you are obsessed about.

Obsession is that burning drive deep down in your gut that, if you listen closely, sounds like someone screaming inside of you. Turning off your obsession by blocking it out with distractions or addictions won't work. Ignoring your obsession to succeed will build up into a quiet desperation, but turning it into the wave of your greatest passion will make you **unbreakable**.

So, while waiting to be motivated is like waiting for the tide to come in before you set your boat to sail, obsession makes you *drag your boat out to meet the water.*

Another big difference between motivation and obsession is that when you're obsessed, you're willing to pay whatever price it takes to make it. The name of the game is called "whatever it takes." You will do anything to top the charts, beat the competition, and push the naysayers aside when they tell you to slow down.

It doesn't matter if you're not obsessed with your dreams yet—you're beginning to understand what obsession is, you've felt it within you a few times, you know exactly what it feels like to have something awaken inside of you and fill you with excitement. Maybe your obsession feels unnatural to you. Maybe it doesn't feel real. But it is real, and it won't go away—it will wait for you to uncover it.

Real obsession for success, the kind that turns Da Vinci or Pablo into world-class artists, or Charlie Chaplin into a world-class entertainer, doesn't just go away. You can ignore it, but once awakened, it reminds you it's there.

Always remember that only *you* are responsible for your success. Nobody is going to save you. Nobody is going to show you how to succeed. Nobody is going to believe in your dreams if you don't. They may support you. They may encourage you. They may correct you. But they aren't responsible for you. You owe it to yourself to be obsessed with your dream and to chase, build and win your best life.

You don't have to "discover" your obsession. You just need to awaken it

You need to know that obsession lives in you, lives in me, and within the thousands out there who are still confused. Many will ignore their obsessions long enough and will burn out that flame. But few will be lucky enough to fully awaken to their obsession, and this is going to include you.

How will you know when you've tapped into your obsession? That's easy. It's all you think about. It consumes your thoughts. You are working on your obsession mentally, even when doing other work for someone else. Obsession is your awakening. It is when your mind is fully fixated on your mission. You know exactly what needs to be done without writing it down or carrying reminders. Your gift of obsession is what makes your inner "beast" come alive.

You need to get obsessed, *now*, with destroying your life on average. You need to get obsessed with shaping your life the way it is meant to be. You aren't going to live your dream life and find happiness by buying more stuff, earning credit at the bank, or taking a dream vacation you have to spend six months working for just to pay off. You're only going to build your dream life by living your purpose, fueled by your obsession, whatever it may take.

You're going to learn how your obsession will help you and how you can fully activate it. It's time to awaken to your fullest potential.

The Power of Obsession

Why does it help to be obsessed with what you want? Here are 8 reasons to develop an obsession toward your best goals.

1. Obsession helps you grow faster

When you think of and work toward one and only one thing, even if you make a ton of mistakes along the way, you'll grow faster, and thus increase your likelihood of success.

2. Obsession drives creativity

When you're obsessed, second best simply isn't good enough. You're insatiable.

You won't accept something until you think it is perfect. Think of Steve Jobs. Think of Elon Musk. Think of Lady Gaga. When you want something badly enough, you'll unleash your creative best.

Obsession gets you to chart your own course. You aren't bothered with what others are doing. You won't be afraid to reject the way things have always been done by the majority.

3. Obsession helps you believe that what you want is going to happen

The more deeply you believe something to be true, the more likely it is to unfold in your reality.

4. Obsession makes you brave

Something wonderful happens with obsession; you stop overthinking and you stop being afraid. You feel more courageous than you ever have before, and it is precisely this bravery that opens doors and takes you places.

5. Obsession makes you more productive

When you're obsessed with something, you're likely to become the most efficient you've ever been, because you want to achieve your goal, no matter what. Your desire fuels all other aspects of your life and makes you operate at your productive best.

6. Obsession helps you focus

A laser-like obsession is a secret of the most successful people on earth. There's no room for distractions—even with regard to different areas where your input is needed for work. You're focused on one thing at a time. Obsession makes it easier to say "no" to things that are not aligned with your goal. And that naturally makes you more successful.

7. Obsession makes you responsible

When you're obsessed with something, you're not going to spend time making excuses, blaming others, or dillydallying. You're going to take complete ownership of whatever you want to achieve. You'll find ways to get through your hurdles, whether that requires reshuffling your team, going back to school, or seeking out the right mentors.

You want to become the best you can, as quickly as you can. You've got no time to waste with ifs and buts. Obsessive people are obsessive learners; they never stop experimenting and improving their skills and tactics. They take complete responsibility.

8. Obsession gives you a competitive advantage

Say you're up against more talented competitors. You'll still beat them if you outwork them, and to outwork them, you need to be obsessed with what you're doing. Most people give up as soon as things start to get tough. The obsessed don't. They are the few who make it through while others fall by the wayside.

It always helps to remember that all of us are created equal—it is our efforts, passions, habits, discipline, and choices that differentiate us, and all of these can be fueled by obsession.

Your NPP Obsession Building Kit

Now that you know what it means to be obsessed and why it's important in chasing your dreams, it's time to learn exactly how to build the obsession to become great. You'll find several action prompts below that will help you activate your obsession. You can become a master at one or learn to excel at a handful of them.

1. Decide that what you want is possible, no matter what it may be

No matter how impossible something may seem to you at the outset, your passion will make it probable, and then possible.

When Elon Musk said, "We're going to Mars" or when Walter Disney envisioned a happy world, it seemed impossible. They then fought all odds to make their vision a reality.

2. Set big goals – you'll figure out how to get to them

If you were to reverse engineer your future, what would it look like today? What is the biggest goal? Ask yourself if you could have anything, what would it be? What have you always wanted? Write down your goals. The bigger and scarier, the better. It just means you'll level up to reach them.

3. Give yourself permission to chase your dream

You should need no validation or permission to chase any of your dreams—they are yours and yours alone to believe in and bring to life. But if you still need permission to begin, I'm giving it to you right now. You have no time to lose. You don't know what will happen next week. You need to begin chasing your dream today—you've waited around to see what happens long enough.

4. Relentlessly chase one goal at a time–be prepared for resistance

The time for hedging is over—it's time to commit to a single course of action with all you've got. Your chance to succeed increases with your level of commitment because it parallels an increase in effort and knowledge.

If you have a clear goal, you'll build a clear strategy. Calculated risk is not harmful, recklessness is.

5. Focus on what you want every single day

Visualize your goals. Focus is power, and it is the difference between hitting your mark and coming close to it. Do you want to "almost succeed," or do you want to "hit your mark" head-on? Focus channels your thoughts and energies to make it happen.

6. Use journaling to build clarity

Start keeping a journal and write down your goals, not just once but every day. Repeat your goals to yourself and write them down so many times that they become a part of you. You'll be better able to identify what you really want because it's in front of you and not in your head.

Only a small handful of people reach this level of clarity, passion, and commitment. Maybe 1% of the 1% write down their goals every day. It doesn't matter what you start writing—tap your inner power and remember a time when you wanted something so bad it set you on fire. That fire is still there. You think it's gone but it's not. You can reignite it.

7. Build a system of feedback loops

An important part of developing an obsession with something is to get into the practice of maintaining a feedback loop, whereby you're continuously thinking of how you can improve at something. The world is changing faster than ever before; it's easy to get carried away with a little success, not knowing that the wheel is about to turn. It's important to constantly question any internal biases and reach out to get real feedback.

8. Get rid of fear

Fear and obsession don't go hand in hand—one drives out the other. A small amount of fear is healthy—it shows you that what you're chasing matters to you, and keeps you taking a sensible course of action. Fear encourages you to plan better and to manage risk better. In small doses, it's good for you. But if it's crippling you, you need to address it, now.

9. Leverage the power of compounding

Lastly, remember that extraordinary people are not made in the blink of an eye. It's years and even decades of work that goes in and compounds, along with an obsession to never quit. No matter how ordinary you think you are, getting better by just 1% every day across the aspects of your life you care about the most, whether it's your fitness, emotional health, finances, or creative satisfaction, can take you miles ahead when cumulated. Always remember and leverage the power of compounding.

Everyone's obsession is different. Some people are aware of their obsessions and commit to them, whereas others' obsessions are crowded out by the noise. Listen to what you truly want, and go after it, "No Punches Pulled." You now know how to wake up the beast within.

Chapter takeaways

- You don't need to find or discover your obsession—it already exists within you and has been reaching out to you. You only need to awaken it.
- Obsession and motivation are different. Motivation relies on emotion and is volatile. Obsession is all-consuming,

makes you unbreakable and unstoppable, and gets you to your goals, no matter what it takes to make it.
- Your obsession aligns with and fuels your purpose; it drives you to become a master.
- You want to develop an obsession when it comes to chasing your goals because it helps you grow faster, makes you more creative, makes you more responsible, productive, focused, brave, and gives you an edge over your competition.
- Use as many tools from your obsession building kit as you can. Begin by deciding that anything you want is possible. Write it down. Chase each goal relentlessly, one at a time. Practice journaling. Get feedback. Get rid of fear. And remember the magic of compounding.

THE 6 HABITS OF SELF-CONTROL

*"To handle yourself, use your head;
to handle others, use your heart."*

—Donald Laird

Your head—basically what you know and believe—your mind and heart, are your biggest assets. If you use them right, you become unstoppable. To do that successfully, you need to master the art of building self-control.

So far, you have been doing very well and, this course will accelerate your learning even more once you learn the six phenomenal habits of self-control.

Right now, let's dive in and optimize these habits.

1. Focus on One Habit (and Behavior) at a Time

We discussed this strategy in an earlier section of the book. Why am I sharing it again? That's because when we try to discipline ourselves, we often get carried away by the process. While trying to do too much, or become even better than before, we start to fill up our plate with so many tasks, activities, or various 'good' ideas. That's when you are likely to force yourself to work on multiple habits at the same time.

You may try to quit smoking, exercise daily, work 10 hours a day, increase your clientele, and beat procrastination all at the same time. You may manage to handle this for a couple of days, but your willpower will collapse soon because you are not in the habit of exerting too much pressure on yourself. You will end up frustrated, burned-out, and drift back to the old, familiar habits that exist inside your comfort zone.

That is why you must always start with one habit.

- Pick the area of your life you want to improve first.
- In that area, select any one improvement you wish to achieve. For example, if your health matters to you and currently diagnosed with diabetes type II but are determined to control it, you could work on it.
- Create a meaningful goal based on the improvement you aspire to make. In this case, it could be, 'I want to control my diabetes and control my blood sugar level.'
- Next, identify all the unhealthy habits you currently have pertinent to that improvement you want. If your blood sugar level is exceedingly high, is it because you eat calorie-rich foods, because you don't walk, or because you are prone to chronic stress? There could be other reasons too.
- Make a list of the habits you need to work on, so once you complete working on a habit, you work on the next one in line.
- Once you have identified the key areas that demand your attention, pick one habit you wish to break and replace it with a healthier one.
- Next, create a habit change plan based on it, as taught earlier, and get to work.

- If you want to build a certain habit individually, not necessarily in place of an existing habit, identify the area, create a goal on it, make a plan of action, and get started with it. For instance, if you want to read more books, figure out the kinds of books you wish to read, why you want to do so, have your compelling reasons ready, create milestones, have your action plan in place, and start working on it right away.

After completing a specific goal, revisit your list of habits, and work your way up to another.

2. Create Incremental Goals

Incremental is an adjective that refers to an increase in something. Add this adjective to your goals to turn them into 'incremental goals.' What are they? Well, they are extremely powerful and lend quite a helping hand to you when you embark on the journey to empower your self-control.

I have mentioned a couple of times earlier in the book how your willpower starts to drop unbearably low when you take on a goal as a whole. For example, if someone asks you to read a 600-page book, you will likely go bonkers only thinking of it, let alone opening the first page.

Imagine your brain going through the same problem when you make a public announcement to become sugar-free in two weeks, lose 30 pounds, or quit smoking. These goals may sound immensely big and empowering at first, but in the long run, such big claims mostly make you go through a downward spiral of troubles.

Announcing something big sounds good to your ears and

mind. When you challenge yourself, you feel excited. A surge of adrenaline, the hormone responsible for both stress and excitement, occurs in your body. This adrenaline rush makes you feel elated. However, the rush soon dies down. When it does, you realize how overwhelming the **BIG GOAL** is, and that's when the reality starts to sink in: it is **difficult!**

Usually, in such circumstances, most of us give up. While using different excuses such as your goal being too big, wanting different things in life, or not setting the correct and meaningful goal, you quit it.

In actuality, the problem does not lie in any of these areas. It stems from not making that goal realistic enough. This is where incremental goals come in handy. They make your huge, overpowering goal more manageable and doable. Instead of taking up something tremendous as a whole, you chop it down to make it more breathable.

If someone told you to read two pages of a book every day, naturally, that feels easier to manage. You know it will take you about 15 minutes maximum, and within only 15 minutes, you will have completed the task. On the contrary, when someone asks you to read a 500- page book, it feels pressurizing even if you have about a month to finish the book.

That is why I always focus on setting incremental goals; I advise you to do the same. Here's how you can do that.

- Take your big goal and chop it into a medium-term milestone. For example, if you want to lose 30 pounds in a year, your medium-term goal can be to lose 15 pounds in six months.
- Take that medium-term goal and chop it down into a short-term goal, say lose 7.5 pounds in three months.

- Focus on this short-term goal and further butcher it into weekly milestones to ensure that you have a target to achieve every week. If you wish to lose 7.5 pounds in three months, it means you have about 12 weeks. You could easily lose around 0.5 pounds every week.
- Now focus on what you need to do to achieve that goal. If you decide to lose weight with the help of aerobics, pick a starting point. For instance, you could start with doing aerobics for 10 minutes a day. Then, you need to slowly increase the duration every week to turn it into an incremental goal. Here's how your incremental goals should look like:
  - Work out for 10 minutes 6 days a week in week
  - Work out for 15 minutes 6 days a week in week
  - Work out for 20 minutes 6 days a week in week
  - Work out for 20 minutes 6 days a week in week
  - Work out for 25 minutes 6 days a week in week
  - Work out for 25 minutes 6 days a week in week
  - Work out for 30 minutes 6 days a week in week
  - Work out for 30 minutes 6 days a week in week
- Use this process to keep building on the goal until you start working out for the desired amount of time every day.

As you follow through with your incremental goals, you will start noticing positive results and shall move closer to your goal. Also, this process does not exhaust you because you build up to the desired success instead of pushing yourself too hard and knocking yourself out in the process.

3. Set Clear Cravings Boundaries

Clarity is one of the golden keys to success in any area of your life. The clearer you are on what you want, the easier it becomes to achieve it. How do I say that with surety? Because that's how I have transformed my life for the better in every aspect of life.

When it comes to building self-control, you need to be clear on everything, especially when it comes to setting up boundaries for your cravings. Decide on what you wish to control, why you need to do so, how much of it you should control, and how to go about it.

The clearer your boundaries are, the better you follow them, and the faster you move towards your end goal. Clear boundaries refer to knowing the limits you need to follow and when to observe them.

- Focusing on the habit you wish to change, think of the distractions you are likely to experience.
- If you have already identified them as taught earlier, go through them.
- Analyze every distraction, every temptation in- depth, and think of the boundary you need to have in place. For instance, if you know you will feel tempted to eat a hamburger after two days of not eating it, maybe the boundary could be to eat half a burger on the third day and treat yourself to a full burger when you stick to the diet for a week.

    If you decide not to tend to unexpected visitors during your work hours in your home office, think of how to communicate that boundary to them. Perhaps

you could send off such visitors, not attend their calls, or refuse them politely if they show up.
- Once you decide which boundaries to set, write them down and go through them at least twice daily: once in the daytime and once before going to bed. Checking them when the day starts reminds you of what you ought to do in the day and going through them before dozing off alerts your subconscious to focus on the boundaries better.
- Make sure to revisit your boundaries and check your performance on them every few days. For instance, if you have been refusing to meet friends during your work hours, gauge your sentiments. Has it been easy for you to say no? When has it been difficult? How can you make the transition even smoother? Focus on the root cause, and you'll easily discover the answers.

You will stand astonished at how quickly you skyrocket your success once you start setting clear boundaries and communicating them to yourself and others with more clarity.

4. Make a Reward System

A system of rewards is crucial to progress in life. I discussed rewarding yourself briefly earlier. Now I want to dig deeper into the aspect.

Rewarding yourself is a crucial part of success because it gives you that dose of excitement. It gives you the adrenaline rush and dopamine you need to feel good about yourself.

You already know what adrenaline does to you. Now, let's talk about dopamine a little. Dopamine is the 'reward chemical.'

Both it and adrenaline and many other chemicals are hormones your body produces naturally when triggered by certain outside agents. Dopamine makes you feel good about yourself; it improves your happiness, confidence, and enthusiasm levels. There are four main ways to enjoy a good surge of dopamine:

- Completing a task
- Celebrating little victories
- Engaging in self-care activities
- Eating food

All these four aspects pertain to self-control. When you complete a milestone, your dopamine levels improve. When you celebrate those wins and reward yourself, your dopamine levels rise again.

One common way to rejoice over a victory is to celebrate over a plate of food, which once again spikes your dopamine levels. Moreover, while building your self-control, you are likely to engage in self-care activities that do wonders for your dopamine concentration.

When you engage in these activities, you like yourself better, feel self-motivated and find it easier to stick to your goals and fulfill them.

Having established how rewarding yourself keeps you invigorated, let us focus on creating a reward system.

First, let me clarify why you need to have a rewards system and not just one reward that you treat yourself with once in a blue moon.

Having a rewards system means you set a range of different rewards for different milestones and engage in them every time you achieve a certain milestone. Instead of using the same reward every time, you entice yourself with something fresh and uplifting as you work towards something you truly want to do or achieve. This keeps your interest alive in the journey.

Sadly, sometimes we use a certain reward to the extent that it stops feeling like a reward. For example, because you have a pizza takeout every time you complete a buyer's order that now, it feels routine to you. It no longer excites you, and when it doesn't please you, you stop taking it seriously. That's when you slowly or sometimes even very quickly start losing interest in your goal as well.

Carrying on with this, another mistake many of us make when setting rewards is to use the same prize for every kind of victory. For example, you may go shopping for clothes whether you have lost 5 pounds or 7 pounds or even 20. This also reduces your interest in the goal because it makes you feel as if your efforts aren't appreciated enough.

The best way to handle these issues is to build a foolproof reward system.

- For every habit change plan, you have already identified the milestones.
- Assess the nature of the milestones and how you feel about each target. For instance, working out for 10 minutes a day may not be a huge task. However, since you haven't exercised in half a decade, it could be monumental for you.
- Once you have assessed what a milestone means to you, give it a certain ranking: important, very important, most important, or something along these lines.
- Next, think of some healthy rewards you could treat yourself to after completing the milestone. The rewards

could even be something unhealthy in a controlled amount. For instance, treating yourself to a slice of chocolate cake after two months of healthy dieting and portion control is fine as long as you don't go overboard with it and treat yourself to the entire cake.
- Put down all the rewards in your journal, and describe how valuable they are for you, each at a time.
- Complement every milestone with a corresponding reward based on its importance for you. If going on a week-long vacation is the most valuable reward, enjoy it when you have been staying true to your fitness-based action plan for two months.
- Peg every milestone to a reward and put it down on your calendar—**Google Calendar** is a great app that can simplify your life. Use it for this purpose and to create all your other routine schedules.
- Stick to the reward system and keep a close eye on it. Every time you are close to achieving a target, spend some moments reflecting on what that accomplishment can do for you, and you'll feel even more energized to achieve that feat.

As you implement the fixed reward system, analyze it routinely to check whether it works for you. If a certain reward lacks luster or isn't effective enough to keep you hooked to your target, replace it with something more rewarding.

5. Beware of Triggers and Emotional Switches

Clarity is essential. It matters when it comes to setting your goals and boundaries, and also when it comes to knowing your emotional switches and triggers.

We are bound to experience different emotions in different life situations. Even when we have complete command of them, we experience them, which is good and proper. Our emotions give us insight into how we feel, how different factors affect us, and how our reaction or response shapes our life. As you start to become emotionally aware, aim to understand your emotions very well, including their influence on your behaviors and life.

- After deciding to work on a particular habit, once again, examine how you engage in it, what triggers that habit, and why you stick to it.
- Take each of these three parts of the habit loop and think of the emotions at play in the loop. For instance, if you smoke when your friend visits you, what emotions do you experience then? Do you smoke with him to rejoice, or is it because you want to vent out your frustrations via a couple of smokes with a friend?
- It is okay to pinpoint as many emotions affecting a respective habit as possible. Write them down.
- Also, identify all the possible emotions at play for each of the three: trigger, routine, and reward. An easy way to do that is to ask yourself questions such as: Do I feel relieved when I do this? Or does it help me mitigate stress? Or does it provide me with pleasure?
- Now focus on looking for these possible emotions when you are about to engage in a specific behavior.
- When exactly do you feel stressed before having a smoke? Do you have a headache before that? Or do you feel overburdened, and that looming feeling leads to stress and then smoking?

- Start looking for these symptoms, and when you identify them, start working on managing those emotional cues and triggers.
- Look for ways to calm yourself down. I'll share some valuable exercises in the following chapter to help you out.
- As already discussed, you can also distract yourself with different activities. Emotions that trigger temptations aren't real. Once you distract yourself, you lose focus on them. That's when you need to remind yourself of what you ought to do in actuality to divert your attention towards it.
- Moreover, name the emotion you can feel in that moment and verbally acknowledge that you are experiencing it. You can even write that down. For example, if you are sad and feel like having a drink or two, say, 'I feel sad and want to drink.' Once you have verbally acknowledged that emotional trigger and temptation, take a deep breath and ask yourself if that's what you genuinely want. For example, you could say, 'Am I just tempted to do it, or do I really want it?' Trust that you will get a very clear answer. Now it is on you not to ignore the genuine answer, and instead, oblige it by **not giving into the trigger.**

Like with everything else, keeping track of your emotional cues is crucial as well, so you get a deeper comprehension of which emotions you are getting a better hang on and which ones need more supervision.

6. Focus on the Bigger Picture to get Long-Term Growth and Sustainable Habits

You didn't get to where you are in life within the blink of an eye, right? For anything meaningful to stay in your life, you have to focus on building long-term, sustainable habits. Likewise, you cannot empower your self-control, build powerful habits and reclaim your life with the snap of your fingers.

When you try to become healthier, build a long-term commitment to it. If you want to become physically fit, don't just think of losing the extra 10 pounds, but focus on building muscle strength. Don't stop working out or eating healthier once you reach your desired weight, but inculcate that habit for the long run, ensuring it stays with you and ensures you stay in the best possible physical, mental, and emotional state.

Here are some key ideas to focusing on the bigger picture to create long-term growth

Always keep your core values in sight. Go through them at least a couple of times every week and ask yourself if you genuinely follow them. If you get 'no' as an answer in any one area, think of what you may not be doing right and how you can fix the issue.

Keep building on your compelling reasons every week. You know how to dig them out, right? Carry out that practice regularly to ensure you identify more reasons why you wish to achieve a goal and empower your self- control. We are constantly changing: the situations, experiences, and different nuances we go through in life influence us. That means our compelling reasons should change too, sometimes not entirely, but in intensity or form with some modifications.

Perhaps you may now feel strongly about making moments in your life count and living healthier now that you have seen a friend lose her loved one. Maybe now that you sense body pains, you realize how important it is to give up on fast food and eat healthier. Our compelling reasons are open to change. Accept this reality, then commit to revisiting and building on them over time to identify more reasons why you need unwavering commitment to build or break a respective habit.

Make visualization a constant part of your life. Everyday, think of making it to the finish line. Play that video in your head repeatedly, and when you see yourself becoming triumphant in the end, focus on the particular emotion you experience in that time. Name it.

Is it confidence, happiness, excitement, trust, joy, exactly what? Now, you need to anchor the emotion to a certain gesture, such as snapping your fingers, pressing two fingers, tapping your arm, or anything else. This is a neuro-linguistic programming (NLP) technique that helps rewire the way you think and feel.

You anchor that emotion with the respective gesture, such that every time you practice the gesture, you experience the particular emotion. This technique allows you to feel happy, strong, confident, etc., all within a couple of moments.

Ensure that you practice the chosen gesture a couple of times when thinking of the emotion to anchor the two successfully. Now try the gesture and sense if you can feel the emotion. If you don't feel it right away, go through the steps again. Every time you feel like you are losing your grip over your emotions, envision yourself making it to the finish line and try the anchoring technique; you'll regain your strength and get back on track.

These six habits of self-control are what you need to get everything in order. You can do it all if you work on all of these, but please remember to do it one by one. To do that right, supplement the process by managing your energy, exercising, and relaxing more often.

BUILT FOR STEALTH: A BRIEF CONCLUSION

Now that we are at the end of this brief journey, I would encourage you to read back through the material again by investing just 15-minutes a day first thing in the morning.

Choose a chapter or key principle to focus on—for that day or the week—and take a few minutes to read through it, implementing the strategies as you move through your day.

Remember this: Your life is the sum efforts of every decision you make. Or don't make. By making a strategic decision to do something, to be someone, or to live your life a certain way, your mind begins to find ways to create this journey.

You are not just existing in space. You have been granted the keys to the universe. The doorway to everything you dream of doing and being is waiting in front of you. You only need to use the key to unlock that door and step through into a new way of life.

What are you waiting for? There is no guarantee that tomorrow will arrive. Make your opportunity now.

As we step into unknown territory, I'll leave you with these words from legendary poet **Robert Frost**:

> I shall be telling this with a sigh
> Somewhere ages and ages hence:

> Two roads diverged in a wood, and I—
> I took the one less traveled by,
> And that has made all the difference.

See you on the other side of that door,

Scott Allan

Rupa - 241
10/7/23